No Place Like Home: The Tent City Diaries

NO PLACE LIKE HOME:

The Tent City Diaries

~

COSTA MANTIS

~

Snapdragon Books

Cover design by pro_ebookcovers

Book design by katsatori89

Snapdragon Books
Westlake Village, CA
805-901-4305
www.snapdragonhealingcenter.com

Library of Congress Control Number:

ISBN: 978-0-9672875-4-6

10 9 8 7 6 5 4 3 2 1

To my beautiful granddaughters, Katie and Emily.
We can change the world with love.

How can I expect you to listen to God,
if I don't?

Acknowledgments

My heart overflows with gratitude for the love and kindness I received from others on this journey.

Thank you, Sister Libby, Greg Bunker, Boyd and Christina, Earnest and Landa, John, Tracie, GP, Paula Lomazzi, Rev. David Moss, Steve Watters, Mark Merin, Cathleen Williams, Maureen and Cliff Black, Joan Burke, Justin Wandro, Tamie Dramer, Mike Edwards, Scott Levin, Terri Kline, Moe Mohanna, Garren Bratcher, Deborah Greaves, Rena Fulgencio Landaker, and so many more who gave so generously of their love and support.

Thank you, Sherry Hursey and Rick Cowling for your friendship and love, and helping to engineer my companion audiobook with impeccability and grace.

Thank you, Maureen Hoyt for your meticulous editing and encouragement.

Thank you, Shari Hollander for your never-ending energy and passion to share this story.

Thank you, Snapdragon Books and Valerie Kobabe, for your infinite belief and love in my work, and helping to end homelessness with your amazing healing work at Snapdragon.

Thank you to my beautiful family, especially my dear daughter and son, Megan and Bob. I count my blessings for one of the greatest gifts in my life, your joyous, generous, enduring love.

Thank you, God, for calling me to do this work.

Thy will be done.

" As a man changes his own nature, so does the attitude of the world change towards him. This is the divine mystery supreme."

~ Mahatma Gandhi

"When you really listen to yourself, you can heal yourself."

~ Ceanne Derohan

Wednesday, April 1st

~

"What is wrong with those people?"
"Why don't they get a job?"
"They're all lazy alcoholic drug addict bums!"

~

It sucks to be unloved.
Human beings thrive on love.
To be homeless in America is to be stigmatized, misunderstood and unloved.

~

On the drive up the I–5 to Sacramento, I must have said the 23rd Psalm for two hours straight. "Yea, though I walk through the valley of the shadow of death, I will fear no evil…"

Then I called my dear friend, Scott.

We've been friends for 30 years. We've made movies together, been in business together, gone broke together, and I know no man who is kinder, more compassionate, or has a bigger heart than Scotto.

"I don't know what the hell I'm doing, Scotto. I'm on my way to "tent city." I'm moving in. Today. Me and my camera. In a tent. I've never done anything like this, bro. I ain't no journalist, jack, I'm an artist."

"I know how you feel, Cos, but you'll do fine. Everything in your whole life has led you here. You help others in your work and in your life. That's what you do. This is who you are. It's what makes you special."

"Thanks. I hope you're right, bro. I'm feeling pretty out there. Exposed. Vulnerable."

"I'm sure, but what you're doing is absolutely amazing and needs to be done. Come on, you lived in Times Square. You had homeless people sleeping on your doorstep. Or pissing on it. They were your neighbors then. They'll be your neighbors now."

"Yeah, but I wasn't living in a tent then. I've got to film and edit and file reports every day and post them on youtube. I've never done anything like this before. At least in Times Square, I had a roof over my head and a flush toilet!"

"Hey, I know. I'm not saying it's going to be easy, but if anybody is prepared for this journey, it's you! Your whole life has prepared you for this moment."

My whole life has been preparing me for this moment?

Me moving into "tent city" to live in a tent with homeless people?

What a moment!
I hope he's right.

~

I am moving into a homeless camp of 300 people.

I am going to live as they live, in a tent, no water, no bathroom, and no electricity.

Thank you for standing by me, Lord.

I can't do this without You.

So, some research and my Divine Guide led me to Loaves and Fishes on North C. Street in Sacramento, CA. to speak with the head nun, Sister Libby.

~

A week ago, March 24th, I was sitting in the dentist chair. Admittedly, it's a strange place to receive Divine Guidance, but that's how it happened. Sitting in the chair, I received a message from God to "give the homeless a voice." Or maybe it was just my dentist talking while I was under novocaine.

I began online research that afternoon and took to the road the following morning with my camera gear to document a homeless camp in Ontario, CA.

Two days later, I was on the road again to homeless camps in Sacramento, CA, and Reno, NV., observing, filming, scouting, and gathering info on the ground, face-to-face with anyone who would talk with me.

I barely scratched the surface in those three days of scouting, yet I was deeply moved by what I saw.

Overwhelmed is more like it.

Disturbed, distraught, confused.

Saddened, bewildered, angry.

My mind was spinning, but my heart was clear.

I had no answers, but I knew I had to do something.

My first stop was Ontario, CA.

A "tent city" is there behind a razor-ribbon topped cyclone fence. The fence is to keep out "violators", I was told by a security guard. A "violator" is someone without a camp ID, not "certified" as a resident of the camp. It is managed by the Sisters of Mercy in Ontario and policed by private security. Security also told me I can't do any filming without a permit from the city and permission from the Sisters.

Why are homeless people behind razor ribbon?

Oh right, to keep the "violators" out.

But it looked more like a concentration camp than a safe place for displaced Americans who need help.

I never thought of America as Nazi Germany before.

My early research revealed that a high percentage of the homeless, 50% or more, are mentally challenged or mentally-ill.

Razor ribbon for the mentally-ill?

In America?

Really?

I found that confusing, disturbing, and unsettling.

I was in shock!

I drove over to City Hall but decided to forego permits for the moment.

I went back to the camp and did some discreet drive-by filming from the car just so I would have my first shots in the can.

~

Next stop, Sacramento.

There was no razor ribbon there.

Thank God.

But no toilets or water, either.

Over 200 tents on the dump site of Blue Diamond Almonds,

4

over 300 people with nowhere else to go - mentally-ill, disabled, displaced, veteran Americans we call "homeless," down by the river on the wrong side of the tracks.

Not exactly a KOA campground.

From the top of the levee, overlooking the sprawl of hundreds of random tents across the flatland and treeless acres of almond shells, I was overwhelmed again and wondered if I was really up for this mission from God.

There is so much human suffering here.

I feel small, scared, and insignificant.

I'm one man with a camera.

What can I do?

How am I going to "give the homeless a voice?"

I'm glad I didn't bring my full camera package; it would be way too conspicuous and premature for a first scout. I'm a stranger in a strange land here, and I don't want to stick out too much. Instead, I brought a pocket camera for stills. I took a few wide shots of the scene.

"What you takin' pictures of? You got permission for that," an angry voice calls out from a tent.

"Oh, I'm sorry. No problem. These shots are not for publication. They're for research," I answer back in a non-threatening tone, hoping to ease any potential tensions.

"Do your research somewhere else. Don't be takin' no pictures 'round here, asshole!" yelled the angry voice.

I put my camera back in my pocket and strolled on, trying to be cool and appear non-threatening. I didn't want any trouble. But I can't help thinking what kind of reaction I'll get when I bring my big camera out.

Help me, God.

I wouldn't be here if it weren't for You.

See, I made a personal deal with God 20 years ago that anytime He called, I would listen and obey. So, when He said "give the homeless a voice," I packed my bags and got to work.

But right then and there, faced with this real and present anger and hate on the ground here in "tent city," I was filled with doubt and fear.

Overwhelmed in my mind with gnawing visions of hurt and hate, anger and violence I did the only thing I knew to do. I prayed. And I prayed more.

I slept in my car that night. I parked on C Street in front of Loaves and Fishes under a tree to dim the glare from the streetlight. A security guard came by at some point in the night but didn't bother me. I guess he couldn't see through my tinted windows.

No one was around at 2:00AM when I ran across the street to use the porta-potty.

Sometimes, it sucks getting old and having to go to the bathroom in the middle of the night. Especially when you're sleeping in your car.

It must really suck being homeless - and old.

~

I hit the road at dawn, headed east on Interstate 80.

Next stop, Reno.

The majesty of the Sierra Nevada Mountains were breathtaking, stark contrast to the wasteland in the rear view of my mind. The snow-capped peaks and tall proud pines gave me hope. No anger or hate here. I could breathe again.

Reno, nestled in the shadow of the Sierras, was a neon oasis in the high desert red rocks.

Mountains and neon; nature and glitz; casinos, high-rollers, and homeless all come together in Reno.

The center city archway proclaims "RENO, THE BIGGEST LITTLE CITY IN THE WORLD."

The sun was setting as I rolled into town so I did a quick scout, grabbed some beauty shots on the strip, and found my way to Reno's homeless community while it was still light.

The Salvation Army has built a beautiful new facility. Out front on the sidewalk, people were laying out cardboard padding and putting up tents to keep them warm in the anticipated chilly night slipping down the slopes of the Sierras.

Too cold for me.

I found a Motel 6 for $27.99 for the night. I turned up the heat and took a hot shower.

People could freeze to death on a night like this.

~

I was up before dawn to catch the daily morning cycle of Reno street life when the homeless folks rouse with the break of day. It was so cold I could see my breath.

Did you ever sleep on concrete?

When the temperature was below freezing?

If you haven't, you should try it sometime.

It might just change your thinking about easy it is being homeless.

Who in their right mind would ever choose to be homeless? Who would choose to sleep on frigid, hard concrete on a freezing night instead of a warm, soft bed inside with heat and plumbing?

Maybe that's the key.

Is anyone here in their right mind, or do they have a choice?

The normal, regular, working, non-homeless people look at homeless people and think *"Why don't those lazy bums get a job? Why don't they work? This is America! Get a job!"*

Did we ever stop to think that "lazy bum" might be a vet with PTSD; or a mentally ill woman suffering with schizophrenia; or a lost soul with bi-polar depression; or a guy disabled by physical injury; or a family evicted because they can't pay their rent because they lost their job in the worst recession since the Great Depression?

Do we ever stop to think that "lazy bum" may not be a lazy bum at all but is a distressed human being who is not able to work because of an illness or disability we cannot see and may need help, understanding, compassion, and love?

Not usually.

What I noticed is that many of us are afraid of "those homeless people, those lazy bums." We roll up our windows and lock our doors. We look the other way. We change lanes to get further away from them. We cross to the other side of the street.

We pretty much do everything we can to avoid contact with homeless people at any cost, as if their plan is to harm us or infect us with disease.

What if we took a different approach? What if we look at them as fellow human beings who just need a little help?

What if we approached them with empathy and understanding instead of judgment, and discarding them as worthless souls?

I'm not saying rush out and hug yourself some homeless folks. Some of them may need a shower first.

I just can't help but think that in the richest country in the world, where we can send people to outer space and create Facebook and google, can't we come up with a better way to treat our veterans and help our mentally ill and disabled than dumping them on the street to fend for themselves?

Surely, a think tank in Silicon Valley funded by the Gates Foundation and assorted billionaires can generate some viable plan for helping the less fortunate in America.

Is Mother Teresa the only one with enough compassion to care for the needy?

It breaks my heart to see so many veterans on the street.

When a man or woman serves this country and puts their life on the line, we owe them more than an honorable discharge. If they return from service with PTSD, bipolar disorder, CTE, physical or mental disabilities, whatever the malady is, we need to help. They've served their country. They deserve the best help money can buy. We owe them that.

I took some shots of life on the streets in Reno and headed home to Southern California.

I had plenty to think about and review and many hours on the road to reflect.

The open road and the hum of tires would give me space and time to ponder how I'm going to tell this story of homelessness in America on film.

~

How am I going to show homelessness to people who don't want to see it?

~

I grabbed my trusty road atlas and surveyed my travel options: Am I going to return the same way I came, back through Sac or take a different road down the eastern side of the Sierras?

I pass on the Interstate and take the road less traveled through the eastern valley.

A detour up a mountain with a switchback-winding road was perfect for reflecting on the data I had collected on the three sites I visited – Ontario with the razor ribbon, Sacramento with the tents, and Reno on the street.

Nearing the top of the mountain, I pulled over for a few moments to soak in the view.

Nature always makes me feel good. Standing there looking at the snow-capped mountaintops, ragged rocks, steep slopes, and towering pines, I breathed in the fresh air. Nature is strong and good, simple and clear, honest and real, animals and plants in balance and harmony. My tense shoulders eased, and I felt at home. God is here and all is well.

All the conflicting thoughts in my mind about which city and which homeless community to showcase made me question what can one man alone do - with no backers, no sponsors, no money, no crew ?

Just me and God.

Standing in Mother Nature's domain, in all her splendor and glory, I felt peace and serenity. The answers will come.

I prayed.

"God, thank you for calling me to give the homeless a voice. You are right. These people need to be heard. But I am feeling lots of doubt and am filled with uncertainty. I'm not sure I can do this alone. Or even do it at all. How am I going to help veterans and the mentally ill? Thank You for guiding me and showing me the best way to serve You and serve the homeless with love and compassion. Thank you for removing my fear and doubt and filling me with strength and courage. Thy will be done."

I breathed deeply and filled my lungs with clear, crisp mountain air and felt refreshed, confident God was with me and would guide my way.

I am never alone.

God is with me every step of the way.

That's what I told myself anyway.

~

I saw that a short detour on Route 341 would take me into Virginia City.

I grew up watching TV as a kid and "Bonanza" was one of

my favorite westerns. The closest town to the Ponderosa, the Cartwright ranch, was Virginia City.

I took the detour.

Glad I did.

The road less traveled.

Virginia City was a living movie set. It's an old mountain mining town complete with saloon, sheriff's office, boarded sidewalks, and cowboys!

Yippee-kay-yay!

If you covered the paved streets with dirt, buried the phone lines, and hid the tourists, it's an authentic period set.

I was filled with the amazement of a child, expecting a shootout in the street. Or to see Little Joe and Hoss Cartwright ride into town.

Virginia City seduced my imagination with a titillation of childhood memories and a playful distraction from my uncharted work ahead.

~

My mind was whirling, the wheels humming and rolling beneath me on the road.

As a film producer, I was taught to get at least three quotes for every line item, at least three prices, three locations, three options before making a final decision.

My three choices were clear. Now, I needed to make the final decision: Ontario, Sacramento, or Reno?

Aristotle says that storytelling is all about conflict. Without conflict, there is no drama. Without drama, there is no audience.

Ontario has razor ribbons and the look of Auschwitz.

Reno has casinos and neon, wild west ruggedness, and street grit, an ironic contrast of high-rollers and homeless.

Sacramento is the state capital and the city fathers are about to evict the homeless from "tent city," even though all the shelter beds are full and the homeless have no place to go.

Ever since Lisa Ling's report broke on the Oprah Winfrey Show, Sacramento's "tent city" has become the hot media story of the moment. International news crews are rushing to "tent city" to send stories home to hungry audiences in Rome, Tokyo, Paris, Beijing, and beyond.

This is not good news for Sacramento, the capital city of California. Pictures of Americans living in third world squalor with no water, no toilets, and no help is not the image California, the 9th largest economy on planet Earth, wants to project to the world.

"Tent city" has to go.

~

The answer is immediate and obvious.

I have to film the conflict.

Prayer and logic lead me to the same conclusion.

I have to go to Sacramento.

The decision is made.

~

Now, how am I going to pay for this project with no sponsor and no backing?

I can't afford a motel.

Do I stay in a tent with my camera gear?

What am I going to do for food and water?

Where am I going to shit and shower and brush my teeth?

Where am I going to charge my batteries and phone every day?

Where am I going to edit and upload to youtube?

What do people do when they lose their jobs and lose their homes?

Where do they go?

Where are they supposed to stay?

What ever happened to the basic human rights of shelter, water, and sanitation in America – for American citizens?

We always respond to earthquakes, tsunamis, and wars in other countries around the world with overflowing generosity and compassion.

Isn't it time to take care of our own veterans and mentally ill right here at home?

How am I ever going to give the homeless a voice if they don't want to talk to me?

So many questions, so few answers.

All I know is, I'm going to Sacramento.

~

I had a long drive home to figure all this out.

Or some of it anyway.

~

I felt like Christopher Columbus, Neil Armstrong, and Odysseus all rolled into one.

An adventurer on a voyage, a mission, a leap of faith off the cliff into the unknown.

What discovery will this mission provide me to give the homeless a voice?

~

I popped a Bob Dylan CD into the player and let my mind sail into the unknown, exploring the myriad possibilities on the road ahead, cruising south down the eastern slopes of the Sierra Nevada Mountains.

The open road was the perfect place to free my mind to wander into the unknown future ahead.

~

Got home.

Cut a two-minute video.

Told my daughter and son-in-law and my two little granddaughters I was moving into a "tent city" in Sacramento, and I would be away for a while, maybe a month.

Told my sister.

Told some friends.

I did *not* tell my mother, too much to explain over the phone. She's on a "need-to-know" basis anyway, and she doesn't need to know her artist son is going to live in a homeless camp. It would only give her more to worry about and yet another way to vent her disproval.

I didn't tell my brothers; they might slip and tell mom.

~

My daughter, Meg, and her husband, Bob, cooked dinner for me.

I am so blessed with a fantastic relationship with my daughter, son (in-law), and granddaughters. When my first granddaughter Katie was born, I moved to CA to be closer to enjoy the spills and thrills of being a granddad.

Four-year-old Katie and one-year-old Emily made me green foam hearts with sparkly letters.

I told them I was going to produce and post daily video reports on youtube and call them "Live from Tent City." They made me one heart that read, "Live from Tent City."

The other heart said "We Love You, Papouli." Papouli means "dear grandfather" in Greek. That's what they call me.

What a send-off! Hearts made by my angels to hang in my tent and road food – a basket full of healthy nuts and bars and munchies in case I got hungry on my adventure!

~

Is it really such a wise and prudent thing to move into "tent city" – alone – living in a tent with my expensive camera gear?

"Are you sure about this, God? Giving the homeless a voice? It all seems a little risky to me."

I waited and I listened.

I got no answer.

No hordes of frogs.

No swarms of locusts.

Not even a black cat crossing my path.

Not a single sign.

I chose to trust God anyway and took the giant leap of faith into the unknown.

~

I got off at the Richards Avenue exit and drove directly to Loaves and Fishes.

I knew where to go.

I have been here before.

~

C Street is a long block of brick warehouses that have been transformed into a hub of services for the poor and needy. Everything! There is a daycare and school, medical services, a mental health clinic, a food warehouse, a commercial kitchen and cafeteria to feed 1,000 hot lunches a day, a triage nurse, a spiritual counselor, an addiction and recovery center, housing for abused women and children, a women's counseling and empowerment center, and a beautiful park, Friendship Park, a safe haven for homeless to get off the streets on weekdays from 7:00am to 3:00pm.

All of this is the work of the Sisters of Mercy and Loaves and Fishes.

~

I park outside of the admin building and walk straight upstairs. Behind the reception desk is a small, fit, gray-haired woman in glasses.

Her nameplate reads "Chris Delaney."

I introduce myself. "Hi, Chris. My name is Costa Mantis. I'm a filmmaker, and I am moving into "tent city" with my camera gear, and I need some help."

"All right. Let me call Joan."

Chris calls Joan who appears almost immediately. These ladies aren't messing around, very buttoned up.

Joan stuck out her hand, "Hi, I'm Joan Burke. Why don't you come down to my office?"

I did. I told her my story.

I even showed her a two-minute short I had cut from my scouting trip.

Joan was impressed. "Let me call Sister Libby."

Thank you God for guiding my steps.

Sister Libby appeared in Joan's doorway with a burst of radiant energy and stuck out her hand, "I'm Sister Libby, the executive director of Loaves and Fishes. How can we help you?"

I told her my story about God calling me "to give the homeless a voice."

I showed her my video and told her of my intention to move in and film and file "Live from Tent City" reports every day, to create public awareness, and hopefully generate public support for the homeless.

~

I came to shed light on the human suffering right here in our own backyard.

I don't know where it's going to go.

I don't have a distribution deal with a TV network.

I don't have a backer or a grant.

I'm here of my own free will on my own dime.

I'm simply doing what God has called me to do.

When it comes right down to it, all I have is my camera, my faith, and my heart.

~

Sister Libby got it.

"So, what do you need from me?"

"Well, I need a safe place to park my car for the next month or so."

"We can do that. What else do you need?"

"I need a place to charge my batteries every day. I need a space where I can set up a table and chair and edit my daily reports 4–6 hours a day, every day, 7 days a week. And I need a place to get online to upload the completed reports to youtube."

"We can do that."

Direct. To the point. Decisive.

We hugged.

Me and Sister Libby.

"We're glad you're here. If you need anything else, you let me know, okay?"

I nod.

"Come with me."

I was in shock.

I only just met this woman.

No references or introductions.

Just me and my work.

She listened to me and looked me in the eye and saw my heart and said yes, unhesitatingly and unequivocally.

She had no doubt.

I knocked.

The door opened.

I asked.

And Sister Libby answered.

This must have been Divine Intervention.

I said good-bye to Joan and she, too, thanked me for coming.

~

I followed Sister Libby down the stairs and across the street to Friendship Park.

"I get so many calls a day from the media now since the Oprah show. Calls from French TV and Italian TV and Australian TV and English TV, but none who plan to move in and live in a tent. What you're doing is something very different."

"Thank you, Sister. I think we have to walk a mile in another man's shoes if we're going to tell his story."

"Well, we're glad you're here."

"Thank you, Sister."

At the front gate of the park, Sister Libby told me to wait right there while she went over to talk to a big guy by a little green and white shed that said "Day Storage."

They talk for a few minutes, and I drink in the setting with my eyes.

The green and white paint on all the buildings matches Sister Libby's green vest and green hat.

I notice a smattering of green hats and vests throughout the crowd.

There must be several hundred homeless men.

Bushy beards.

Ragged shoes.

Scruffy hats.

Worn backpacks.

Lots of bicycles.

Lots of suspicious eyes, all looking at me, the stranger in their midst.

I'm glad I don't have my camera gear. That could be way too confronting.

I'm feeling anxious and uneasy. Thoughts are racing through my mind.

You made a big mistake here, brother.

Do you really think you can do this?

Can you live in this hurting land of suffering and homelessness?

All of a sudden, I'm not feeling so sure and confident anymore.

~

"Costa, I'd like to introduce you to Boyd. This is Boyd Zimmermann."

We shake hands.

"He will take you out to "tent city" and help you get set up. If there's anything else you need, you let me know. God bless you and thank you again for coming."

Sister Libby hugs me and leaves.

"Yes, Sister Libby."

It is like God has provided me one of his very own angels to guide me and watch over me in this unknown land, that has the hair on the back of my neck standing up.

Boyd is a big hulk of a man who doesn't talk much.

He doesn't seem too happy about having me thrust upon him, but it doesn't look like he is going to say no to Sister Libby.

He's stuck with me.

If Sister Libby entrusts my life to Boyd, so be it.

All I can do is trust that Sister Libby and God are doing me right.

~

Boyd and I park at the end of Dreher Street where a bike trail leads into the woods.

I pop the trunk. I put on my backpack filled with my camera gear; I bungee-cord my tent, sleeping bag, sleeping pad, and tarp onto my rolling suitcase handle; I put my tripod over my shoulder and lock up the car.

"Need a hand?" Boyd asks.

"I'm good. Thanks."

At the crest of the hill, "tent city" comes into view. It's just as I remember from my scout.

High-power lines tower over the landscape, train tracks, the river, a levee, and there are tents as far as the eye can see.

The bike path up the hill turns from paved to gravel. My rolling luggage can't take the uneven rocks and potholes and tumbles over, spilling the tent, sleeping bag, and pad sprawling onto the dirt.

So much for not needing a hand.

Boyd watches me re-pack and re-bungee my gear, looking around, like he's embarrassed by my clumsy bumbling and doesn't want to be seen with a klutz like me.

I can't tell if he's disgusted or just getting a good laugh at my struggles in this strange land.

~

It's not easy being homeless, moving all your possessions around with you wherever you go every day.

That's why "tent city" is such a safe haven. They don't have to move every day.

And maybe even more importantly, there is a community of friends watching out for each other, helping each other through these extreme and challenging times.

~

Boyd helps me set up camp next to him, just the way Sister Libby requested.

I meet his fiancé, Christina.

I meet their friend, Discovery John.

I tell them my story, including my mission from God, to give the homeless a voice.

John is wary.

"A lot of these people are going to be very suspicious of you. They don't trust the press. It isn't going to be easy. Most of them won't want to talk with you."

"I understand that and expect that. But I am not the press. I am not here to sensationalize or take advantage of anyone. I'm here to give the people a voice, but everyone will have to sign a release. I will not film anyone without their written permission first. I'm here on my own to give the homeless a voice, and hopefully create awareness to help change the way we handle the homeless, mentally-ill and disabled here in America."

"Well, it all sounds very nice. But it isn't going to be easy."

John obviously speaks with many years of street knowledge and wisdom. His mannerisms and diction give the impression that he is highly educated, well-read, and very smart.

"Thank you, John. I appreciate your honesty. Thank you for whatever help you can give me."

~

My little tent is cozy.

I have a flashlight hanging from the center so I can write at night.

The foam stars Katie and Emily made for me sit next to my pillow.

They make me smile and warm my heart.

Here I am.

In my tent.

In "tent city."

All alone.

Kinda scared.

I don't know whether to cry or throw up, but neither would be cool. It would make a very bad first impression with my new neighbors. Haha.

It is what it is.

This is only the first day.

What the hell have I done?

Thursday, April 2nd

An earth-shattering screech jolts me awake.

Oh, my god, what is that ear-piercing sound?

It sounds like shrieking pigs at the slaughter. A giant saw cutting steel. Fingernails on a chalkboard. The hair on my neck is standing on end.

It's just the 2:00am freight grinding through "tent city," squealing brakes, shooting searing rocket-sparks from its wheels into the homeless night.

I guess this is my welcome wagon, screeches of death at the whirl of a giant killer saw.

Even with my padded mat, it's cold out here on the ground.

I put my ball cap on and pull the sleeping bag over my head.

It's just a freight train, but I'll never forget those screaming brakes.

What have I done?

~

I hear Boyd and Christina talking, but it's still dark. I fumble around and find my phone and flip it open – 4:47 in the morning.

Boyd told me they get up early to go to work at Friendship Park, but I didn't realize it would be this early.

It's cold, and I don't want to get up. I can't film in the dark anyway.

I pull my bag over my head for all the warmth I can get and curl up into the fetal position.

~

I hear every sound now. My senses are on high alert.

I hear gravel crunching. It sounds like wheels rolling on a pebbled path. Too light to be a car. No engine sound either. Probably a bike. Or a rolling cart.

Zip!

That has to be a tent flap opening.

Dawn is breaking.

It's getting light out.

My cell says 6:16.

~

I pull my jeans into the sleeping bag and slip them on over my long johns.

It's warmer dressing inside the bag than out in the chilly dawn air.

T-shirt, long underwear top, long sleeve turtleneck, flannel shirt, four layers on top, two layers, jeans and long johns, below, cap and hood pulled tight against the morning freeze. It's so cold I can see my breath.

The first thing I have to do is find a place to piss.

Boyd said I could do it on the other side of the levee.

After that, I usually like to take my morning dump.

But not this morning.

Pee only, thank you.

It's a lovely place to take a leak.

Scenic "tent city" on the banks of the sparkling, pristine American River.

~

I set my camera and tripod up on the levee to get a high and wide establishing shot of "tent city" at dawn as it comes to life.

It's the morning march, a migration across the sprawling urban wasteland. By ones and twos, a few threes and fours,

24

people appear out of tents, heading west over the tracks to Loaves and Fishes for bathrooms, hot coffee, and a roll. Breakfast for hundreds in the safe haven of Friendship Park.

When I pan my camera from the natural beauty of the river to the distant towers of commerce, here is "tent city" sandwiched between nature and city.

How can this be?

From the natural beauty of the sunrise over the American River to the third world conditions of "tent city." The contrast is stark.

Is this what America has become today?

Are we a land of contrasts and divisiveness, the haves versus the have-nots?

What ever happened to the land of the free and home of the brave, welcoming the "poor and huddled masses" of the world to our very shores with open arms?

Does that verse at the base of the Statue of Liberty mean anything anymore?

Or has it all been garbled and whitewashed in politically-correct gibberish?

Where are all the humans in this mess?

~

Ronn is my first interview – tall, broad shouldered, bushy brown hair, wearing an insulated plaid work shirt.

I have him sign a release.

He is fine with that.

"What happened, Ronn? How'd you end up here in "tent city"?

"When the economy crashed, they stopped building houses. I'm a carpenter. I moved in with my dad for a while. I could only stay there so long. I've been here a month now. It sucks. That's all I've got to say. But the people here are nice. At least it's safer than being on the streets."

~

I asked myself, how many millions of builders and tradesmen have been impacted by this "recession"?

I don't know the difference between recession and depression.

What does it take for an economy to be in a depression?

Right at this moment, people seem pretty depressed right here in "tent city."

Does that make it a "depression?"

~

Seeing a big guy like Ronn who looks young, strong, and healthy and yet he's homeless, I think to myself, why can't this guy get a job? He's healthy. Surely, he can do something!

Perhaps he suffers from mental illness but it's not my place to ask.

~

When economies crash, millions of people lose jobs.

What happens in one person's life without a paycheck?

What happens when a whole family loses its paycheck?

Most people lose everything they own – cars, homes, credit.

And now they're homeless.

I don't know much about economics, but all I know is this kind of economy sucks.

~

How long has it been since I've had a paying job?
November of '08.
Now, it's April '09.

Money's getting tight.

What's going to happen if I don't find an angel for this project?

Am I going to end up homeless like the people I came to interview?

God, you've got to be kidding.

Right?

~

Michael's story is totally different.

He didn't want to be filmed on camera but he talks openly. I guess he just wants to talk.

"You might say that I'm responsible for my homelessness. That would be true."

"I would say that my life has been a series of bad decisions I made since leaving home at sixteen. I worked. I got jobs. But then I'd hang with the wrong people or get in a fight or do the wrong drugs or get in an accident, whatever. It was just another wrong decision on my part. So, I'd move on to another place, another job, another chance hopefully. I came out here to California a year ago 'cause I heard there were jobs in Sacramento but that was over a year ago and I still haven't gotten work. This is the worst it's ever been looking for work. I could always get a job. Not now. It's different. I stayed at Cal Expo for a while. Then I had to leave there. Now I've been in "tent city" here on and off for a couple of months. Sometimes, I stay with a friend over by the mission."

~

Michael left home at sixteen.

I wonder what was going on at his home that made him think that life on the streets would be better than life at home?

At sixteen?

~

I'm standing here talking with strangers, homeless Americans living in tents - no running water, no sanitation, nothing.

They've lost their jobs, their homes, their lives.

They've lost their way.

They're refugees in their own country - no place to call home.

~

These are people who need a lot of help – now!

Right here in our own backyard.

No shelter, no water, no sanitation.

I thought every American had shelter, water, and sanitation.

Don't we need to take care of our own, right now?

~

I strap my camera pack on, grab another, smaller backpack with short sleeves and shorts, in case it warms up later, shoulder my tripod, and join the morning march to Loaves and Fishes.

~

Friendship Park is mobbed.

Hundreds of men, a few women – many of their eyes are on me and my camera. Their stares are not welcoming.

I nod and smile. I have my pack on my back and my camera, boom mic and tripod on my shoulder. Someone finally asks, "What channel you with?"

"I'm independent. I moved into "tent city" yesterday. I'm shooting a documentary about life in "tent city," but I won't film anyone without their permission."

"Cool."

"Thanks."

Not everyone is happy about me and my camera.

"Don't be filming my ass. I don't want no cameras around here."

This guy is troubled.

"I respect that. I won't film you."

"Got dat right."

"Yes, sir."

"Don't sir me."

"Sorry."

"You bet your ass, you're sorry."

Spotting Boyd at the Day Storage shed, I make a beeline for him. Maybe I'll feel safer close to Boyd.

~

Men line up at the Day Storage shed to store their gear for the day.

Hauling fifty to sixty pounds of stuff around the streets all day gets heavy.

Boyd gives every man a smile, a hug, and a number. I set up to film Boyd at his shed, close up at first, so as not to film anyone else.

A couple of guys agree it would be okay to film their backs as long as I didn't film their faces.

I film some wider shots of Boyd checking in the two guys at the shed.

"Thanks, guys."

~

Feeling a little calmer and a little braver, I head over to the breakfast line.

Christina volunteers at the Park, serving donated, day-old donuts, cakes, and rolls, smiling at every customer and wishing them a blessed day.

I ask the other volunteers working with Christina for permission to film them in the background. They all nod agreement.

I capture some of Christina's natural kindness and cheeriness on film.

~

I love making movies, making art, telling stories in pictures and sound.
I count my blessings that I can follow my passions, telling stories and making art from the heart, to make the world a better place every day.

~

Not only did Sister Libby give me Boyd and Christina to watch over me, she also gave me an office at Friendship Park, where I can edit and charge camera batteries during the day while the park is open.

The office is just up the steps from the Day Storage shed, so Boyd is close by within yelling distance if I have an emergency.

A big green canopy covers a large wooden deck attached to a converted construction trailer with four doors. I'm door number three, next to Nurse Susie on my right, the triage nurse in Friendship Park.

To the left is the homeless newspaper office. The door on the end is Pastor Linda's office, offering counseling and comfort for whomever knocks.

~

Thank you, Sister Libby, for your generous heart and this special place to work.

~

The room is 6'×8' with a door, a window, three desks, six stacking chairs, a light switch, and outlets on two walls. I do my Feng Shui and made it all orderly and "safe" for creating.

When I create - film, cut, write, edit - I open my heart, my mind, and my soul to the Universe and everything going on. I want the place where I create to feel warm and safe for so much personal openness and vulnerability.

I make it so. I put two desks and two chairs on the right wall. I put the third desk on the left and stack the other chairs in the corner.

I make a galley, desks on either side, open down the middle.

I can put my Macbook Pro, drives, camera, and battery chargers on the right desk.

On the other desk, I place the camera backpack along with clothes, snacks, and my white canvas National Wildlife Federation bag that serves as my briefcase.

My LL Bean satchel was too upscale for this project.

No need for LL in TC. Tent city.

When in, do as.

I lock my camera and tripod in the office and hike over to get the editing gear out of my car which is parked in the lot, across the street, behind Loaves and Fishes.

I have a ton of heavy gear to schlep every day, and now I have free, safe and secure storage for my car (and my editing gear in the trunk), and an office with power for editing.

Thank you, Sister Libby!

Humping my gear back to the park, I think this must be what it's like being homeless and having to carry everything you own with you all day long. It really sucks.

~

I've set a personal goal for myself to post a report on youtube every day, for as long as it takes to find a positive resolution to all this unnecessary suffering called homelessness.

This translates into filming B-roll and conducting interviews every day; securing signed releases from each person I film every day; digitally capturing, viewing and logging every shot on paper every day; writing, filming and recording voice over every day; writing the outline for the story every day; editing footage – 1–2 hours – down to a 2–3 minute short every day; adding music and mixing sound every day; adding titles and credits every day; compressing the finished file for internet streaming – every day – all by 3:00pm when the park closes. And lastly, crossing the street to administration at Loaves and uploading the finished product to youtube by 5:00pm before admin closes; and returning to "tent city" and repeating it all again the following day. None of this takes into consideration normal daily needs: going to the bathroom; brushing my teeth; getting something to eat; praying; and sleeping.

This is my new routine, "Live from Tent City."

Solo.

Solitary.

Alone.

Just me.

~

And millions of men, women, and children, all homeless, every single night, right here in America, without shelter, food, water, and sanitation.

My daily youtube reports will hopefully begin to educate the American public about the trials and tribulations of homelessness and life on the street and stimulate positive public reactions.

Then, maybe, just maybe, with awareness, we, the people, collectively will find a solution to help others less fortunate than ourselves.

Maybe.

~

Love works miracles.
Helping others is the right thing to do.
Always.

~

After just one night of "research" in "tent city" by the tracks, waking up without a place to go to the bathroom, being homeless is definitely and unequivocally not camping.

~

Yes, it is my choice to live in the heart of the beast of human suffering and depression here in "tent city," but now more than ever my purpose here is clear. I must persevere in the face of adversity and keep the dream alive.

~

A knock at the door startles me.

I look up.

It's Boyd, looking through the window of the door.

I keep the door locked because he told me to.

"Trust no one," Boyd said.

I get up and let him in.

"You goin' to lunch?"

"Is it now?"

"Nah. 'Bout a half hour. How's it goin' in here?"

"Good."

I don't usually have strangers walking into my editing room, but this is hardly my usual situation, and I actually welcome his company.

"You wanna see what I've got so far? I mean, it's just rough, but you'll get an idea."

Boyd nods, and I cue up *Live from Tent City: Day One.*

I have already laid in some music as well as the opening titles. It's about a minute and a half long.

Boyd watches closely until the picture stops, and the screen goes to black.

He nods.

"Whadya think?"

"Good. I'll come get ya for lunch."

He leaves the editing suite.

The sensitive artist in me wants more feedback., but the door is closed.

I get back to work.

I have a deadline anyway.

3:00pm today.

No time to waste. Time for feedback later.

Work.

Time is of the essence.

~

Boyd bangs at the door.

"Bring your camera; it may not be safe here."

I trust him to be my guide and don't question his judgment.

Sister Libby told him to take care of me, and he does.

I lock up. Christina is waiting at the bottom of the steps, leaning on her cane. We walk to lunch together – Boyd the hulk, Christina with her cane, and me with my camera.

~

The lunch line forms down an alley, around the back of Loaves and Fishes, through a traditional arched Italian brick walkway, complete with a fountain of St. Francis and his birds.

There's a woman on a stool taking lunch tickets by the door.

Boyd tells her I'm Sister Libby's guest.

"Thank you for coming."

She clicks the counter in her palm, counting every guest served at Loaves and Fishes.

"We feed anywhere from 700 to 1,000 every day at lunch. Employees get to eat first so we avoid the lines and can get back to work." Boyd chuckles.

There's a double-decker stainless steel counter before us with stacks of black cafeteria trays, napkins, and silverware. On the other side of the counter are five or six aproned volunteers, dishing out rolls, salad, vegetables, lasagna, dessert, milk, juice, and coffee.

Helpful volunteers in red vests walk the lunchroom floor, refilling beverages and providing baggies to anyone who wants to pack their "leftovers" for an evening snack back in the tent.

What a wonderful thing Loaves and Fishes is doing here, helping the needy get food and services, comfort, and compassion, while treating every single person with dignity and respect.

~

I feel very conspicuous with my camera and tripod on my shoulder.

"What channel are you with?" asks a smiling man in glasses and red vest.

"Not with any channel. I'm independent. I moved in to tent city yesterday. Sister Libby made Boyd watch out for me."

Boyd chuckles and smiles.

"Well, you're in good hands then. Thanks for coming." The smiling volunteer goes on to help others.

"And thank you for serving lunch to so many people," I tell him.

I grew up in a family restaurant, so I know what it takes to feed 1,000 people.

Here at this facility, they serve 1,000 people every day – for free!

Sister Libby told me they raise over $4 million every year to provide services for the homeless, all from donations.

~

I follow Boyd and Christina to a pine-plank table with six chairs.

They join hands, offering their other hands to me. I hold hands with them, and Boyd prays over our lunch.

"Heavenly Father, thank you for these blessings here before us that we may be of service to You by serving others. And thank you for sending Costa to "tent city." In Jesus' name, we pray. Amen."

"Amen."

"Thank you, brother."

I felt I was more of a burden and nuisance to Boyd since he was obligated to take care of me because Sister Libby said so.

I didn't know he cared.

I'm touched.

~

We are joined at the table by a young woman with wild, wavy, red hair and fire in her eyes, a ring pierces her bottom lip. My guess, she's Irish American, 30- or 40-something.

"Hey, sistah," Christina sings out.

They embrace in a hug and a kiss.

"This is Elise. This is Costa. He moved into "tent city" yesterday." Christina introduces us.

We shake hands.

"What's with the camera?" Elise asks.

"I'm here to give the homeless a voice. I'm hoping my videos might help shed some light on the whole subject."

"Well, that all sounds good and high and mighty, but I'll tell you one fuckin' thing, you ain't one of us. You can fucking come here and live in a tent but when this is all said and done, and they come in and shut down "tent city," we will still fucking be here but you won't. That is the fucking difference!"

With that, Elise smacks her hands hard on the table and leaves.

"Don't mind Elise. Irish temper," Christina reassures me.

~

I understand, but how could I not be affected by Elise's tirade?

The anger, resentment, and suspicion in her accusations are heartfelt.

Setting up my tent last night, I could feel that same energy with everyone's eyes suspiciously wondering who the new guy is.

That same tense, guarded feeling is there as I walked into the park this morning.

I keep telling myself I'm on a mission from God and not to worry about all the bad energy. With God's protection, none of the icy stares can hurt me.

But I still worry.

It still bothers me.

And kind of scares me, too.

"Yea, though I walk through the valley of the shadow of death, I will fear no evil . . . "

~

My afternoon editing is productive, and I finish "Day One" – my very first report from "tent city" just as the park closes at 3pm.

Boyd stops by twice to see the latest cuts. Each time, he watches with intense interest and seems pleased.

~

Across the street at administration, I get online and make a rather clumsy first post of "Live from Tent City: Day One" on youtube – for the whole world to see.

Now, we'll see what America and the world thinks of the situation in "tent city."

~

Something must be done.
There must be change.
This human suffering right here at home is too much to be ignored.

~

I pack up my gear to head back to "tent city" with a sense of accomplishment, and hopes of "Live from Tent City: Day One" going viral overnight!

I'm a dreamer. That's a fact.

I like to dream big.

~

When a tornado strikes and destroys everything in its path, we respond and rush in with aid and provisions: food, water, shelter, medical supplies, mental health help - everything.

When war ravages a nation, we care for the refugees.

When Mother Nature annihilates, we care for the survivors.

The only difference here is that "tent city" is a disaster made by a crashing economy instead of a giant wave.

When the American economy crumbles, how do we care for our own people in need?

~

Leaving Loaves and Fishes after 5:00pm, I go down the stairs and turn left out the door.

I'm loaded with a 50-pound camera backpack, clothing/ snack/water backpack, editing briefcase, and a graphite, fluid head tripod.

I walk a block and go left down the alley past the local fire station to the parking lot behind the Loaves warehouse complex. I pack my editing gear in the trunk and lock up.

"Live from Tent City: Day One" is in the can and posted on youtube, and now, it's on to Day Two.

~

I hike east one block on North C Street, take a left on Ahern, a quick right on McCormack for a long block down to 16th Street.

16th Street is a major artery out of the city. It's five lanes wide and backed up for blocks in the evening rush hour. With all my gear on my back, over my shoulder, and in my hands, I weave through the idling drivers to Dreher Street.

At the corner of 16th and Dreher is The Capitol Casino, Restaurant and Bar. There are two police cars parked out front.

Are the police having coffee, playing craps, or here on an arrest? I wonder.

After resting a minute at the corner, I continue down the block.

~

Dreher Street is a long block, like a New York City cross-town block – even longer with 60 pounds of gear. I stop and rest several times.

~

Imagine doing this every day, hiking city streets with a backpack and rolling luggage, and black garbage bags stuffed with all of your belongings every day.

This is the first full day for me, and I'm already having reservations.

~

I'm doing my best to keep a positive mental attitude in this situation which, on the surface, doesn't appear all that positive.

So, I pray a lot.

I'm praying right now as I hike back to "tent city."

Instead of focusing on the pain and suffering, I keep thanking God through silent prayer, for helping me and guiding my steps so I can be of help to others.

Thank you, God for hearing my prayers.

~

I keep telling myself I have nothing to fear as I crest the hill into "tent city."

Best I can tell, most of the people here are angry and irritable, and they don't really much care for me or my camera.

So, I pray.

Prayer and meditation give me peace of mind and a sense of calm in the middle of the storm.

Prayer may not be the popular choice in most circles these days, but it works for me.

~

The "wasteland", named "tent city" by the media, is an old almond waste landfill, rumored to be toxic because processing almond shells releases arsenic as a byproduct.

I don't know. I don't have a research staff or assistants to confirm or deny. It's all hearsay, but that's what I've heard.

At any rate, it's a dump site under high voltage towers and wires. That can't be healthy.

"Tent city" is buzzing with activity, clusters of people moving about.

A group of guys make an old telephone pole their stoop. I can hear their laughter.

The sounds of people laughing are nice.

A pleasant surprise.

~

Boyd is adjusting ropes, straps, and tiedowns over their tent.

Their tent is actually three tents, arranged together under one giant blue plastic tarp to make their three-room home.

Christina is sitting in her electric scooter with her cane by her side.

Earlier, Boyd told me in the editing room that she suffers from rheumatoid arthritis and diabetes. Sometimes the pain in her knees is so bad, that she can't walk. That's why she has a scooter.

~

The twelve-minute, half-mile hike back here was grueling for me!

I can't imagine doing it with rheumatoid arthritis.

Just another homeless story from the capital city of the Golden State.

~

What can I do about it?
Will my videos make a difference?
So many questions.

~

I put my backpacks in my tent and hang by Boyd with my camera and tripod.

On this project, my camera is my companion at all times.

My gear goes where I go, ready to film at a moment's notice.

Besides, for safety purposes, I can't exactly leave the gear in my tent unattended.

No mistrust of my homeless friends intended.

Just practical production logistics.

It's simple.

I can't film anything without my gear.

So, the camera stays with me.

~

Discovery John rolls up to Boyd's tent on his bike.

John is wiry, windswept, and wild-looking with two graying ponytails, one in his hair and one in his beard. John is lean and trim, wearing shorts and shoes but no shirt. Zero body fat.

Some people might see him as scary because of his wild look, but as an artist, I find him photogenic.

"So, Costa, I hear you met Elise."

I nod, not really sure where John is going with this line of discussion.

"I'll sign a release for your camera and tell you what's on my mind."

"Great. When would be good for you?"

"Right now is fine with me."

"Great. Did ya have a place in mind?"

"Just here in "tent city." You're the photographer. You pick the spot."

I hand Discovery John my clipboard to sign a release. He looks it over and signs one.

I look around for a place to shoot with a "good" background – something that adds purposeful, interesting information to the frame – but not people who don't want to be filmed.

~

When you look at Discovery John, you know right away that he's homeless. He's got the look, weathered and wild. A black nylon lanyard hangs around his neck with a pen, a lighter, and mini-flashlight. In the brim of his worn tan cap is an LED headlight, for night riding on his bicycle. There are bulging plastic bags bungeed to the frame of his bike.

If you're profiling, a backpack plus bicycle plus plastic bags equals homeless.

~

John rolls a cigarette as we talk.

"This is only the tip of the iceberg of what's going to happen. We are living in a false economy of over-inflated real estate that is based on consumption. Credit has tightened and consumption has ceased. They've stopped building houses. What's a carpenter, roofer, electrician, or plumber to do? This "tent city" isn't all from the crash; it's been building for years. Yes, you have people here who lost their homes when they lost their jobs and couldn't pay their mortgage anymore, *and* you have people who have been here for years, so you have both."

If I closed my eyes and just listened and couldn't see John's worn face and mangy beard, I would think I was listening to an economist on the evening news. I thought maybe that was how he got his nickname "Discovery" because he is so bright and articulate, he could be on the Discovery channel, but it's because he lives on an island in Discovery Park.

"What's the solution, John?"

"Safe Ground is the solution."

"What's 'Safe Ground'?

"Safe Ground is a place like this, where people can actually have a secure place to leave their belongings, a place with no drugs, no alcohol, no violence, but with running water and sanitation, a place where people can begin to get their dignity back and go out and look for a job. When you're homeless, you have to spend all your time protecting what you've got and looking for a place to sleep where you won't be rousted by the police or harassed by drunk teenagers looking to "bum-wrestle" you, or club you to death with bats while you sleep. Safe Ground is exactly that, a safe place where you don't have to worry about being harassed, where you don't have to worry about where you're going to stay tonight, and you can begin to get your life back together. It's impossible to have a stable and secure life if you're always on the run. That's like being a refugee in Afghanistan."

Here I am filming this leathered river rat in "tent city" Sacramento, and he's offering a partial solution to the homeless crisis. He's suggesting a way to catch people before they fall too far, a way to help these ill and broken people begin to rebuild their lives. He wants to get them into a safe place where they can begin to heal and rehabilitate, before they are shredded by life on the streets.

John's Safe Ground concept sounds like a logical and reasonable solution.

When people need help, help them.

Instead, the police are called to move those "homeless bums" from the neighborhood, all paid for on the taxpayer's dime.

Where are they supposed to go?

"If I understand you correctly, John, you're saying that if there was a Safe Ground, then you wouldn't have homeless people in random doorways or pushing shopping carts throughout the city. They would have a place to go where their property would be safe. Am I understanding you correctly?"

"That's exactly what I'm saying!" John exclaims as he exhales a plume of smoke, emphasizing his point.

"How much does Safe Ground cost and who pays for it?"

"That's just it. What does it cost to send police out every day to roust people and keep moving them? Look at the money already being spent on harassment. Why not reallocate those monies to helping people instead of harassing them? These are American taxpaying citizens here in "tent city." This is their only housing because they have nowhere else to go. The shelters are full."

John turns and points up the levee to construction machines and dump trucks.

"Look, right now, over there, the city is spending $1,000,000 to make a dog park where people can walk their dogs. $1,000,000 dollars! What kind of shelters, water, and sanitation could we build for $1,000,000 dollars?"

"Quite a lot, I would guess. What about current shelters like the Salvation Army and the Mission?"

"Have you ever been to one of those shelters? They tell you when to wake up. They tell you when to leave. They tell you when to turn your light out. You can't take your pets. You can't stay with your mate. You can't leave your belongings. They have security guards to keep you in your place. They tell you when to sleep, eat, wake up, and leave. What kind of way is that to get help? It sounds more like a prison, if you ask me. The media talks a lot about third world conditions out here, but what about second world conditions. Do you know what that is? That's the KGB. That's what it's like staying at a shelter. The Sally (Salvation Army) has a 60–90 day waiting list, and you can only stay 30 days once you do get in. The overflow shelter out at Cal Expo is full and their guards are even worse. And at the mission, you have to strip naked in front of the security guard, then shower before you go to church and listen to their preaching for an hour just to get fed and a bed. We are American citizens! We deserve dignity and respect too!"

I don't have an answer.

"The "normies" think homeless people are just a bunch of lazy alcoholics and drug addicts. Last time I looked, there is a high degree of alcohol use, prescription drug use, and recreational drug use in normal culture, too! When you get sick, what do you do? You go to the doctor. The doctor prescribes you a pill. What do you think happens when you end up out here on the street? First thing you want to do is self-medicate. Wouldn't you? People out here are in shock when they crash land in Hooverville. You can see it in their eyes. They can't believe they're really here, that they're really homeless. Like returning soldiers in shock, their lives look nothing like they used to look. It takes months to accept the painful reality that you are homeless."

I nod my head. Discovery John keeps rolling.

"You have veterans out here who have served their country and laid down their lives. They were trained to kill. They watched their brothers die, and they survived. They come back and can't adapt. Now, they call it PTSD. You have schizophrenics out here, people with mental disabilities people who were abused since childhood, people disabled from job injuries, everything from carpenters to nuclear physicists. The city can build a dog park, but they can't provide safe shelter for American citizens in need. We're not looking for a handout; we're looking for a hand up. And now the city wants us to leave the "wasteland" with nowhere to go. Where are we going to go? This is madness. We need Safe Ground. And we need it now!"

~

I have come here to give the "Discovery Johns" of the world - these people - a voice.

Surely, someone will see my posts on youtube.

Tomorrow, they will hear John speaking and making total sense.

Someone watching will have a piece of land or money or both, and they will step up and offer it for Safe Ground.

There is the power and the possibility for the internet to reach millions instantly.

Anything can happen.

I still believe in miracles.

Friday, April 3rd

Sunrise on the American River, morning light rims the craggy treetops and turns the sleepy river silver.

I turn my camera around 180 degrees to capture "tent city" at dawn, with the silhouetted city skyline, towering in the distance.

This will be a talking head shot of me delivering my narration with "tent city" in the background.

I hear the approaching sound of bicycle wheels on gravel, and I look over my shoulder.

"Get the fuck out of here with that camera. I'm gonna fuckin' kill ya if I see ya here again."

He flips me the finger and keeps on riding.

He probably thinks I'm just another random news guy here to take advantage of the homeless.

Or maybe he hates his life and is just pissed at the world.

Or is in pain.

Or is schizophrenic.

Or maybe he's tweaking.

I feel compassion for his struggle and empathize with his pain and anger.

But I feel unsettled with his hate and anger, projected towards me.

I hope someone tells him I'm one of the good guys.

I would have yelled for Boyd to help, but he and Christina left 45 minutes ago for Friendship Park.

I hate to live in fear, God, but I really want to live another day and see my granddaughters grow up.

~

I finish my voiceovers – looking over my shoulder – trying not to show my fear.

I pack up my gear and make the pilgrimage to Friendship Park for breakfast and editing, without any more threats along the way.

~

Christina is all smiles on the breakfast line.

I meet Pinky and some of her co-workers.

"Would it be all right if I film some shots of you serving breakfast? I'm filming a documentary."

"Sure, it's okay. Go ahead."

I film some close-ups of Christina as well, serving muffins and smiles.

~

It is my intention to get these stories out onto the worldwide web every day, to create greater awareness about America's "homeless" problem, and generate solutions for this horrible atrocity of human ignorance and indifference.

Denial is not going to fix mental illness.

Looking the other way is inhumane.

~

Boyd pops into the editing room to check on my progress.

I tell him about the drive-by bicycle threat this morning.

"I'll talk to him about it. People know better than to mess with me around here, and when he knows you're with me, you'll be fine. I don't want you wandering all around the wasteland without me, okay?"

"Thank you. I appreciate your watching out for me."

"Hey, Sister Libby told me to watch out for you, and whatever Sister Libby says, I do. I don't want you going anywhere without me – or at least without me knowing where you are. Understood?"

"Yes, sir!"

"I'm not kidding. There are some crazy people around here, and I don't need you to be walking into some meth camp and getting killed. Nobody'll mess with you if you're with me."

"Thank you. I really appreciate it. I just don't want to be a burden on you."

"You're not a burden. Just listen to me. Sister Libby told me to watch out for you, and I'm gonna watch out for you!"

"Thank you, brother. Thank you, Sister Libby."

~

I have another productive creative day in the editing room and have a finished cut of the second installment of "Live from Tent City: Day 2" by 3:00pm, when the park closes for the day.

I leave the park loaded down with my editing and camera gear and cross C Street to Loaves and Fishes admin to upload the finished, edited, mixed, and compressed file of "Live from Tent City: Day Two" to youtube.

~

Thank you, Sister Libby for providing me a place to edit, electricity, access to the internet, security for my car, and gear. And thank you for my guardian, Boyd.

Thank you, God.

~

Done. I stash my editing gear in the trunk of the car, shoulder my backpacks, close the trunk, lock the doors, shoulder my tripod and camera, and make the trek back to "tent city."

~

I count myself extremely blessed growing up with the loving parents I had. Not only did they teach me to help my neighbor and practice the Golden Rule, but they taught me about PMA – positive mental attitude.

Positive mental attitude was a way of life for Jim Mantis. Pearl and Constantine were devout Christian Scientists, and they believed in the power of mind, and they taught this premise to all their children.

Dad was a fighter pilot in World War II. After the war, he had big dreams to strike out for California, but returned home to Reading, Pennsylvania to run the family restaurant, The Crystal. He ran for Congress in 1960. He was a man of action, a take-charge guy with a smile, a kind word, and always with a positive attitude. He gave me my first copy of Norman Vincent Peale's "The Power of Positive Thinking."

I'm still doing my best every day to live up to the standards he set.

My attitude is how I transform my daily pilgrimage - walking the walk with my homeless brothers and sisters - into a daily workout that is good for my health.

I always try to find the positive, just like good old dad.

But carrying and dragging everything you own everywhere you go could get very depressing very fast.

For those of you who still think that homeless people are lazy bums, I can assure you there is nothing lazy about schlepping and humping all your worldly belongings up and down the street every day.

~

How many miles do you walk each day?
How much weight do you carry every day?

Do you have a place to sleep tonight?

Does it have running water?

A shower?

A toilet?

A bed?

With a pillow?

When you're homeless, you don't have any of that stuff.

How is it we can send emergency shelter, food, water, medicine, and sanitation to refugees in distant lands, yet we look the other way in disgust at our own American refugees, right in our own front yard?

~

I cross the railroad tracks and take in the wasteland below, from the river to the transformers, all the way up the levee, people are about. Camps are abuzz with end-of-day activity everywhere.

Friendship Park closed two hours ago, and there's nowhere safe to go but here among friends on the wasteland. People use the fading light to hang out, talk with neighbors, make dinner, or tidy up their camps, and get ready for night.

That's what you do when you don't have electricity and indoor lighting, you wake up at sunrise and go to bed when the sun goes down.

Bad things happen on the dark city streets at night.

I seek out familiar faces, hoping not to see the guy filled with hate riding his bicycle.

Thank goodness, Boyd is outside his tent puffing on a cigarette and talking to one of his neighbors. As I get closer, the neighbor turns and heads back to his tent.

"Hey, Boyd."

"Hey."

"I hope I didn't scare him away."

"Ya kinda did. He doesn't want to be filmed. I told him you were cool with that so please, don't film him. Okay?"

"Absolutely. Thank you for putting in the good word for me."

"Just don't let me down. What are you up to now?"

"I was going to put my gear down and then see who wants to talk."

"Stay close by here in our camp where it's safe just in case anything happens."

"Yes, sir."

"Would you stop calling me sir?"

"Yes, sir."

Boyd shakes a fist at me in jest as we have a good laugh.

I head back to my tent.

~

Boyd is my protector.

He is genuinely concerned about my welfare.

How comforting to know that someone is watching out for me.

I am a stranger in a strange land, but I am not alone.

Not only do I have a guardian angel in "tent city," but a new friend as well.

~

With my camera on my shoulder, I head towards Ronn and a group of guys sitting on some logs.

"Hey, Ronn."

"Hey, movie guy. You're back."

"Yep. Made it back. I'm over by Boyd and Christina."

"You're staying in a tent?"

"Yeah. I'm old school. Walk a mile in another man's shoes kind of thing."

"Cool." Ronn turns to his friends, "This is the movie guy I was telling you about. I can't remember your name. What is it you're doing, a documentary or something like that? Well, you tell 'em."

"Hey, my name's Costa." I extend my hand.

"Hi, I'm VJ."

"Nice to meet you, VJ."

VJ is in T-shirt and jeans and has a three-inch wide American flag bandana wrapped around his high forehead and thinning sandy-blond hair.

"Hey, I'm Phil."

"Hey, Phil, nice to meet you."

We shake hands. Phil has a full head of straight long gray hair in a neat ponytail and an equally neat, trimmed, gray mustache.

He and VJ are very clean and put together. They must be fairly new.

Compared to Discovery John, they're night and day on the neatness scale.

"I'm Reno."

"Nice to meet you, Reno. I'm Costa."

Reno is younger with dark brown hair and movie star rugged looks, his eyes hidden behind Ray Bans. He could be straight out of Central Casting. His jeans and sweatshirt are weathered and worn. He introduces me to the man next to him.

"This is Coyote. He's a professional horse trainer."

"Nice to meet you, Coyote."

"Si, senor."

Coyote's brown leather cowboy hat shows years of wear in the cowboy life. His skin is brown, like fine tanned Latin leather, and he sports a scruffy gray mustache. He pulls his horse trainer scrapbook from under his arm and opens it to show me clippings and tell me stories in excited Spanish of his horses and him at Santa Anita.

"Thank you, Coyote. Like Ronn said, I'm making a documentary. In addition to the documentary, I'm also filming and editing short reports every day and posting them on the internet for the whole world to see. I hope it'll make some kind of positive difference."

"I respect everybody's right to privacy so I will only film and interview you if you want to be filmed and are willing to sign a release form."

"That's cool, man," says Ronn, raising his beer can and clinking it with Coyote.

"Want a beer?" He offers a can.

"Thanks, man, I'll take a rain check. Still working," nodding at my camera.

All the guys are enjoying their afternoon high gravity beers. They're happy and easy-going. They readily agree to being filmed and all sign releases.

"This is a nice scene here, a bunch of friends kicking back and having a good time."

"Who said we're friends?"

We all laugh.

Ronn raises his beer and everyone raises theirs.

"To the good times."

How ironic that I am here in a homeless camp, and these men are sharing fellowship, friendship, community, and laughter, as if they loved life and hadn't a care in the world.

Is it the beer?

Or is it genuine community in the face of adversity?

Or is this the self-medication Discovery John was talking about, life on the wasteland, man making the best of the hand he is dealt?

~

Phil was first to be interviewed.

I film him on the far end of the log pile to give me distance from the guys chatter and better sound quality.

"There's no work in California anymore. I'm going back to Pennsylvania."

How many carpenters, roofers, electricians, framers, plumbers, masons, tilers, insulators, sheet-rockers, plasterers, painters, lumber yard workers, factory workers, bankers, inspectors, realtors and others were hurt when the housing bubble burst, and they stopped building houses in America?

Bam! Just like that, everything stopped, not just in California, but all around the world. I heard somewhere that the global economy had shrunk 50% worldwide since the crash.

"Will you get work back in PA?"

"Maybe with my uncle. If not, at least I have family there. I don't know anybody here 'cept my neighbors and drinkin' buddies."

~

VJ is next, in his red, white, and blue headband. He is articulate and well-spoken. He enunciates clearly and precisely.

"I was a corporate consultant for Fortune 500 companies. I owned the big house in Grass Valley, the trophy wife, the beautiful kids. I was living the American dream. Then the economy collapsed, and all the big corporations downsized. They outsourced jobs overseas to cut costs and increase profits for shareholders. They didn't need my consulting services anymore. After six months of no work and sending out over 400 resumes, I couldn't pay the mortgage anymore.

I lost the house. The wife and kids went back to her folks. And here I am."

~

When was the last time I worked with my buddy Mike for one of his railroad clients?

If I remember correctly, it was January 2008, and this is April 2009.

The balance in my checkbook is below two grand, and if something doesn't happen soon, I could be out here like VJ, Phil, Ronn, Boyd, Christina, and John.

Uh-oh, am I heading down the rabbit hole?

~

Reno agrees to be filmed, as long as he can keep his sunglasses on.

I frame an up-angle shot of him with high-power wires crisscrossing the sky as his background, Reno in Ray Bans, homeless in the industrial age.

"There's the contractor here. There's the horse trainer. There's the corporate consultant, all the way down to the waitress and the bellhop. They all used to be somebody, and they still are somebody! They are not worthless. They are human beings! And now the city wants to tell us we can't live here anymore in "tent city" because it's unsafe and unsanitary. About a month ago, just after Oprah, there was a preacher who brought in 10 port-a-johns, and the city made him take 'em out. Now, they want to throw us out. Like we're garbage. Where are we supposed to go? They say they have 50 beds at Overflow, but they don't take couples unless you're married and me and my girl are not married, so we can't stay together. There is no place for us to go. And what about the 300 other people who live here in "tent city" who are couples like us or have pets and the shelters won't let you bring your pet. People's pets are their life."

"That's like taking your best friend away. It's inhumane, is what it is. The city has $3,000,000 to build a dog park, *(I thought Discovery John said $1,000,000 but I don't interrupt)* for curbs, and parking and a place to walk your dog, but they don't have shelter for the people out here or for the hundreds of other people on the street."

~

I mean I love dogs, but how can they make a park for dogs and not house the homeless?

Would someone please tell me what is going on here?

This is America, isn't it?

~

Today, I picked up a fact sheet at Loaves on homelessness, and I was shocked. The sheet said "There are over 3.5 million homeless in America today and 27% are veterans."

That means there are over nine hundred thousand men and women who served their country and laid their lives on the line in the face of enemy fire, and they are on the street with no place to stay.

Over nine hundred thousand veterans?

In America?

My training as an artist is to remain objective, but I'm afraid my training isn't working. I am stunned, shocked, outraged, in disbelief, and mad as hell this is going on right here in the United States of America.

How can this be?

In America?

That's all about to change.

Just wait until my videos go viral, and the public wakes up to see the way our veterans, our disabled and our mentally ill are being treated.

Citizens across America will be outraged.

~

As a child growing up, there were times when a homeless man was in front of The Crystal Restaurant. Dad would go out and bring him in and seat him at the counter for a warm, hearty meal, then wish him God's blessings and send him on his way.

~

Whatever happened to the Golden Rule?
What happened to "Love they neighbor as thyself?"
What happened to America?

Saturday, April 4th

The Union Pacific freight screeches through the dark stillness of the night again around 2:00 this morning.

Except for the train wheels squealing like pigs at slaughter and the angry bicyclist, my first three nights in "tent city" have been peaceful.

No fights, no theft, and no crime.

~

Saturday morning in "tent city" is different than the first three mornings.

There is no pilgrimage.

Friendship Park is closed.

No coffee and rolls.

Come to think of it, I didn't hear Boyd and Christina get up and leave in the dark this morning, either.

They must be sleeping in.

I set up my camera, shotgun mic, and wireless mic outside my tent to film my morning voice over segment I wrote last night for the daily installment today. Boyd groans like a bear, sticking his head out of their sprawling blue-tarped tent.

"What are you doing today?"

"I'm just setting up to record my voice overs, and then I figure, since the park is closed, I'll head over to the public library to edit today's segment."

"On Saturday?"

"Yep. Gotta get the word out."

"You think your videos are gonna make a difference?"

"I sure hope so."

"Huh. Me, too."

I finish the voice over, pack up my gear, load it on my back and shoulders, and hike into Loaves and Fishes to my car, equipment storage and wheels, all in one.

I drive around looking for a place to grab a cheap breakfast before I go to work at the library for the next six hours.

My mind is in overdrive, trying to absorb and process what I've witnessed and experienced the first 72 hours since I began living in a tent.

~

Homeless people are stigmatized in America.

America's a free country and everybody who wants to work works.

So, if you're homeless, you're unwanted.

No one wants to see you, look at you, be near you, get close to you, smell you, or talk to you.

Pedestrians cross to the opposite side of the street if they see a homeless person on the sidewalk.

Drivers change lanes to move further away from homeless at the corner with a sign. Children are told, "They are dirty, lazy, alcoholic, drug-addicts. They're worthless bums. Stay away from them."

You might as well have the plague.

~

When I lived in New York City, there were homeless people sleeping outside my door at night.

My then five-year-old daughter asked, "Daddy, what's wrong with that man?" and I told her "That's what happens when you don't love yourself. That's why you always have to love yourself."

I experienced a lot of rejection as an artist.

If I let it, the rejection will eat away at my self-esteem and wear me down.

Rejection also eats away at self-confidence, and raises doubts about my art, my worth, my talent, and about myself as a person.

Rejection is a way of life for the artist, so I can easily empathize with the plight of my homeless friends.

When are you going to grow up and do something real with your life?

When are you going to stop playing artist and get a real job?

How are you going to support your family?

You'll never amount to anything!

I heard a lot of that in my life as an artist.

I understand being stigmatized, misunderstood, made wrong, put down, and refused.

As an artist, I've felt that my whole life.

As a father, however, I felt love was the greatest gift I could give my daughter.

If I taught her to love herself, then she would be able to face rejection, grow up strong, and see the good in the world.

It all begins with loving yourself.

~

When God said, "give the homeless a voice," it was a no-brainer for me.

I moved into "tent city," with the refugees on the wasteland.

The only difference between me and them is that I keep God first and haven't bought in to all the rejection society hurls at us.

Why all the hate?

I can't help but wonder how we got to this place in America.

I thought we helped others in need.

~

They are people from all walks of life.

Many are mentally or physically disabled.

One of every four is a veteran.

~

Have you ever been in public somewhere and you could *feel* eyes looking at *you?*

That's what it's like being homeless.

I am homeless.

I am unshaved, four days unkempt, covered in wasteland dust and carrying my life on my back.

Everybody stares at me – and *not* in a friendly way.

It sucks when people look at me with disgust, revulsion, and hate in their eyes and hearts.

It's terrible to feel like I am despised and hated.

What did I do?

I'm trying to help make it better.

It's only been four days.

Truth be told, I think all the hate is getting to me.

My heart weeps.

My soul aches.

I don't like it at all.

~

I am at work on the 4th floor of the public library in downtown Sacramento, capturing, digitizing, and logging yesterday's footage.

Have the governor and mayor seen my "Live from Tent City" posts on youtube yet? Surely, they must have.

Let me check youtube and see how many people have viewed the videos.

~

It takes a few minutes to link to the library's internet.

I can't wait to see how many hits we've had.

This is exciting.

I wonder if they've broken 1,000 views yet or maybe even 10,000.

I emailed the links out to my mailing list of 326, and if they each emailed the links out to their lists and then those people emailed it out their lists, it could be well over 10,000 hits.

It could be a lot of views by now.

~

I finally get to youtube and click on the thumbnail of *"Live from Tent City: Day One"* and look at the number of views.

137.

137?

I emailed it out to over 326 of my personal friends and business associates.

That means only 1 of 3 friends looked at *"Day One,"* and they did *not* pass it on to their friends.

There must be something wrong with the numbers here.

This can't be right.

I click on *"Day Two."*

It's a little better, 177 views.

I click on *"Day Three."*

Down to 129.

~

Are you sure about this plan, God?

~

As a people, as a society, as a country, as the great United States of America, what do we do about the millions of homeless people in our own country who need help?

What can you do?

You can say hello.

You can give them a smile.

You can ask them what they need.

You can give them a bottle of water.

You can say a prayer with them.

Or you can look the other way and walk on.

From ground zero at the center of the fallout from the great global financial crisis of our lifetime, the casualty count grows every day.

People are suffering and need help.

I'm challenging my fellow Americas to rise up and take a stand!

~

I post *"Live from Tent City: Day Four"* on youtube.

How can there be so few hits on my videos?

How could my friends and family not have watched them?

Why wouldn't they pass the links on to their network of friends?

Am I just kidding myself and thinking these stories of homeless people are interesting and compelling?

I admit I'm not a journalist.

I didn't come because of facts and figures.

I came because my heart said it was the right thing to do.

I shouldn't worry about the numbers so much.

Just tell the stories.

I hope it's good enough.

It has to be, it's the best I can do.

What am I going to tell Boyd?

Maybe I shouldn't say anything.

Let's give it a few days and see if the numbers pick up.

No sense in broadcasting bad news about myself. Nothing to be gained there.

Maybe I won't say anything to Boyd just yet.

~

The gate to the lot at Loaves and Fishes is locked.

I have to go to plan B, which I devise as I drive.

The issue at hand is security for the editing gear which lives in the trunk of the car and is normally parked securely at Loaves.

This video and editing gear are my life and livelihood.

I can't afford to lose them.

But I don't have funds for an overnight parking garage or cab fare back to "tent city."

Nor am I ready to hike three miles with all my gear back to the wasteland.

I guess I have to trust God to protect the car overnight and that everything inside will be there when I come back in the morning.

Dreher Street is nearly empty.

I park under a street light at the end of the block.

I pack the editing gear in the trunk, put on my camera pack, grab the tripod, lock the trunk and car, double-check the doors to make sure they're locked, and head home to my tent on the wasteland.

~

Boyd and Christina are sitting outside their tent talking with their neighbor, Beck. They see me approaching. We exchange waves. Beck gets up and leaves.

"Hey, how ya doin'?"

"Great, man, great. How about you?"

"Good. Day off. Taking it easy."

"Looks like Beck still doesn't want to be filmed."

"Looks that way."

"Are you up for telling your story before I put the camera away?"

Boyd looks at Christina. "Feel like doing an interview, honey?"

"Oh no, not me. You go ahead, honey. I don't really feel like talking right now."

"I totally understand. No problem. You can stay sitting right where you are if you like, and I'll frame up on Boyd without you in the picture."

I spread the tripod legs, mount the camera, and wire up Boyd with one of my wireless mics.

I roll camera and adjust the shot as we talk.

"How long have you guys been living out here, Boyd?"

"I think we've been out here seven, nearly eight months. That's a long time to be on the streets. I was depressed when we came out here."

"How did you end up out here? What happened?"

"The usual. We were living in Phoenix. We just bought a triple wide, in Peoria, real nice, three bedrooms. I was working, driving a van for a day labor company. When the construction stopped, there was no need for day labor anymore, and I was out of work. My mom and dad wouldn't help me because they didn't approve of Christina. They offered to take over the mortgage payments if I broke up with her. I wouldn't do that. So, we packed up and moved back here. I grew up here. But there was no work when we got back, and we ended up out here. At first, we still had a van but we had to give that up after two months, couldn't afford it anymore and now, we have our tent."

"What was it like when you first moved out here?"

"It was crazy. I was depressed. Christina has diabetes and rheumatoid arthritis so I tried to make it as comfortable as possible for her. When the churches would come out with tents and sleeping bags, I started stockpiling supplies. I knew what happened to us was going to be happening to a whole lot more people, and they would be ending up out here in "tent city," too. I made a nice place for us. We have three rooms under cover. It blew so hard this past winter, though, it blew everything down. I had to re-stake all the tents. That tent over there is where I keep supplies – tents, bags, tarps; I have two bikes in there for me and Christina. I gave Discovery John his tent. I gave Beck his tent. Taco and the couple on the other side of you, I gave them their tents. I started surrounding ourselves with people I knew, peaceable – no fighting, no drunks, no tweekers. She smokes medical marijuana for her arthritis pain, and she has a card for that. I got Ronn his tent. And VJ his. I think I've passed out twenty-two tents so far. God said to help your neighbor, and that's what I'm doing right here in "tent city."

Boyd chuckles proudly. He's clearly pleased to be able to help others and has a great attitude in the face of this present adversity.

"We even have a handicap toilet for her 'cause she can't make it through the night with her diabetes. We got that over at the Goodwill. Three bucks. We got a queen size air mattress in there, a propane space heater in there and a battery-powered TV in there. I've made it as comfortable as I can for her."

Boyd chuckles again and smiles at Christina. He's the king of his domain, a good man providing for his queen.

If they went to a shelter, they would not be able to stay together because they are not married.

"It's tough being out here. A person could fall out here. I just want to get inside. I don't like it out here."

He reaches out and holds Christina's hand.

"But we've done the best we can do with a lousy situation, and I've done my best to help others and to serve God. I just want to hear God say, "Well done, my good and faithful servant.""

"I'm sure he is already saying that, brother. You've helped so many. I'm amazed at what you've done out here."

"It's not me, it's God. He did this, not me."

"Well, I'm sure God is working through you."

"I just want to get inside. I don't like it out here."

Discovery John joins in.

"We used to have port-a-johns but the city said it violated code and only encouraged more people to move to the wasteland. A church delivered ten portable toilets, and the city threatened to fine them if they didn't remove them immediately! The city said it was because the homeless were vandalizing the toilets but the truth is that the city thought the toilets would make it easy for more people to live here. As if people are just rushing to move out to the wasteland so they can live on top of a toxic dump site filled with propylene oxide just so they can have the convenience of a portable toilet! Did you know that propylene oxide or PPO is a carcinogen recognized by the EPA to cause respiratory failure among other things? I hope you enjoy your accommodations here at the wasteland."

"I didn't know that."

"PPO or propylene oxide is used in the pasteurization and processing of almonds."

"Were you a science teacher before the crash?"

"No, I was not a science teacher before the crash. I was a contractor. But I like to stay informed about my environment, especially the one I am living in. The city may publicly say that if there were portable toilets in "tent city," homeless people would come from far and wide to live on the wasteland. But don't forget, there is a reason it's called the wasteland. Oprah gave it the name "tent city." Contrary to popular political opinion, it is not attractive to live like an animal on a toxic dumpsite – with or without a portable toilet!"

A tall, gangly, young fellow in a blue plaid shirt and baseball cap excitedly bursts on the scene. He blurts right in first chance he gets. "Boyd. Boyd! I got the scholarship. At Wyotech. I start Monday. I'm getting out!"

"All right. That's great news, Albert. Way to go, man."

Boyd stays seated, but they do the bro handshake with the fingers, fist bumps, forearms and ugh!

"Yeah. I just found out. I came straight from the school. I couldn't wait to tell you."

"Congratulations, man! I'm so proud of you."

It is a moment of exuberant hope, a young man in "tent city" aching to share his personal victory with Boyd - his mentor, his father, his teacher, and his life coach.

~

I flash on Grapes of Wrath, a memorable book from high school.

A picture of human compassion in the face of adversity. Somehow, the Joads lived through the Great Depression and the Dust Bowl. They had nothing, yet they still shared whatever they did have with someone else in need.

I came to "tent city" because God told me to come.

I also came to find out if human beings still have compassion in the face of adversity, even though they have lost their jobs, their homes, their lives, and are living in tents.

My answer came in the moment with Albert and Boyd.

Yes, compassion is our nature, even in "tent city."

~

The sun is dropping and so is the temperature.

John pulls his sleeping bag up over his head and shoulders to make a giant hood against the chill of the evening wind. He pulls a baggie from a pocket and plucks a chicken leg from the baggie.

"Leftovers from lunch."

I remembered seeing the ladies giving out those baggies at Loaves when I had lunch with Boyd and Christina.

"Is that usually what most people do for dinner?"

"Yep. Loaves and Fishes is really good like that. All the little hostess volunteers offer you a baggie or two for your leftovers. Most of us rely on Loaves and Fishes for hot lunches and doggie bags to meet our basic nutritional needs. That's why it's strategically essential to stay close to Loaves. Some people have bicycles like myself but certainly not most. There is a limit to how far you can walk every day. People come to the park when it opens at 7:00 in the morning. They know they are going to be safe and not be harassed and told to move along at Friendship Park. A lot of people sleep in the park during the day because it isn't safe to fall asleep at night when you're alone on the street with no one to watch your back. It's stressful. They say in the Army that during battle, you have to sleep with one eye open. That's what you have to do on the street, too. Same thing. I do my dumpster diving at night. Fewer people to hassle me at night and it's easier to hide in the dark. So, I will sleep during the day. Now it looks like it's back to the street again. The city is giving us notice. We're out of here. They won't say when. I hear it's the 13th, then I hear it's the 16th. Soon. Very soon. Good-bye, "tent city.""

I listen to and film John with one eye, while with the other eye, I watch the anxiety and despair growing on Christina's face.

Boyd holds her hand. His loving eyes tell her it is going to be okay.

She tries to smile but her face is as gray as the clay and the creeping, encroaching dusk.

~

Yo, God. It's me. Cosi in "tent city." One quick question.
Why the low number of views on the youtube videos?
I just figured with your worldwide influence, we would have more hits.
I'm not really sure what it is you want me to do here, God.
Is there something you want me to change?
Or should I just get used to it?

~

I never did tell Boyd about the lousy numbers on youtube.
He'll find out soon enough.

Sunday, April 5th

"Tent city" is asleep as I crawl out of my tent with camera and tripod in hand and script in my pocket.

The morning sky is streaked with pinks and oranges, splashing their colors behind the web of stark, black winter branches, reaching for the light.

The rose and salmon sky sparkles off the silent black river below.

Birds soar, squawk, and peep, dark shadows darting and diving through the rosy-fingered dawn.

The world of darkness and demons is losing its grip to the morning dance of color and life.

~

Down on Dreher Street, my car is there, no broken glass, no stolen gear, no police report, no hassle, no problem. Yay! What a relief.

Thank you, God, for the overnight security.

North C Street is quiet this morning compared to the frenetic buzz of the previous four days.

The park is closed on Saturdays and Sundays, but the cafeteria at Loaves and Fishes remains open to serve lunch, and some people are already gathering to get their lunch tickets from the green hats.

~

I meet Willy on the street.

He is excited to share his personal story of recovery and rebirth.

I film him in front of Clean and Sober on the south side of North C across from Loaves and Sister Nora's. Willy is six steps up on the porch, and I am on the street below. I frame an up-angle on Willy with the Clean and Sober sign in the background. Clean and Sober is a recovery and transitional living center in Sacramento.

"I was homeless. I used to live down on the river. But I wanted more out of life, and I had to get up off my butt and do something about it! I found God. Right here at Clean and Sober. I quit drinking. I got a job. I put my life back together, and one day at a time, I've been clean twelve years now. I own my own truck. I have my own place. God has been good to me. He gave me another chance. How many people never make it back from the river? I am one of the lucky ones. I thank God and Clean and Sober for that."

Here's Wilfred "Willy" Dunston, happy as can be in his buzz cut hair and plaid shirt, puffing on his Marlboro, telling me how he beat alcoholism and got his life back together.

I love a good success story, especially one overcoming addiction and hopelessness.

Willy gives me hope. He is a living example that one can come back from homelessness.

~

Everyone I talk with in "tent city" is obsessed with where they're going to go when the city runs them off the wasteland.

I'm worried, too.

Imagine not knowing where you are going to stay tonight or the next night or the night after that.

Scientists and psychologists say that moving is stressful. It's on the top five list of the most traumatic events in life, along with loss of a loved one, loss of a job, divorce, and stroke.

The uncertainty of not knowing where we are going to live is weighing heavily on everyone.

Everyone is anxious and on edge.

Faces are lined with worry - cigarettes are inhaled with stress of the unknown.

Uncertainty, fear, and panic gnaw on wearied, worn hearts.

Nerves are frayed.

Where are they going to go?

No one knows.

There are no answers to their questions.

~

Fear is a powerful force.

Fear can save your life, or fear can kill you.

I heard someone say there were over thirty million unemployed in the U.S. and another fifty million under-employed.

What happens when the unemployment benefits run out?

How many millions of Americans are living right now with the fear that they are only one paycheck away from being homeless themselves?

Imagine 80,000,000 people unable to pay their rent.

Good-bye house, hello tent.

The banks still want their mortgage payment, recession or no recession.

Visa still wants you to pay for the stuff you bought when you had a paycheck.

Lose your job and life is uncertain.

Lose your home and life is frightening.

Lose your car and life is radically changed.

Lose your self-worth and ... you fill in the blank.

Falling from the security of job and home to the insecurity of the street is shocking and terrifying for anyone.

Imagine if it happened to you.
It is akin to being a refugee from war.
You had it all.
Now you have nothing.
And now you have to deal with fear on top of all that.
Talk about overwhelming.
Will you ever get your life back?
Or will you die homeless?

~

After Willy, I interview Adam.

Adam probably played fullback in high school. His shoulders are broad, his neck thick. He sports a mustache and wears a black ball cap with Jesus in the shape of a fish embroidered in green on the crown. He speaks eloquently and is well-versed in the Bible. I'm guessing he's a preacher.

"Money don't make you; God makes you. You can have all the money in the world but when you die, and God takes you home, you don't see no Brinks truck behind no hearse. You can't take it with you. Down here, people have no money, yet they are helpful, courteous, and kind. Money doesn't make you happy, God makes you happy. People need to come down here and see what life is without the bling. You never know, they might even learn something new."

On the street, the artifice is stripped away.

~

You can't brag about the size of your house anymore – ain't got one!
You can't impress with a fancy car anymore – bank took that, too!
You can't flash your gold card no more – credit denied!
Everything's gone with the drop of a pink slip.
Imagine that.

We humans don't like change.

Change ignites fear.

Change leaves us in the darkness of our thoughts.

We like it better when we can control things.

Change the channel, change your mind.

But when you're homeless, you can't change a damn thing – 'cept your attitude.

~

People are seriously stressed-out, uptight, and short-tempered.

Everybody's having a hard time controlling their attitudes right this moment.

No one knows what's going to happen.

Fear's got the best of them.

The stress of their unknown future weighs heavily.

People are jumpy, paranoid, on guard.

When are the cops coming?

Some are angry.

Some are scared.

Some are dazed and confused.

Some are paralyzed by fear.

Some just weep.

All are irritable.

Everyone knows their final days here are numbered.

Their homes and community are about to be destroyed.

And there is nothing they can do about it.

Like hurricane Katrina.

They feel helpless.

They feel under attack at all times, not knowing when the next wave of destruction will strike.

People are being forced out.

Where will they go?

They don't know.

Scatter and cover.

Every man for himself.

You've got to get by on your own now, no one to watch your back, no place to leave your personal stuff while you go to lunch.

Driven off the land like their dust bowl forefathers, no jobs, no homes, no place to go.

What are they supposed to do now?

Where are they supposed to go?

~

You want to talk about mental torment?

Take away a man's job away, take away a woman's home.

Dump them on the street, and watch what happens.

Now, we've got reality TV!

And the reality is, it's too painful to watch.

~

I load up my gear and drive to the library to do my thing.

Charge my camera batteries.

Digitize, log, and capture all the video and sound.

Define the story.

Lay in the voice over I recorded earlier.

Select shots and edit the pictures to tell the story.

Add and place credits and subtitles.

Add and mix sound track music.

Compress the finished edit for streaming online.

Log on to the internet and upload "Live From Tent City: Day Four" to youtube.

Pack up.

Hike back to car.

Return car to Loaves lot.

Stash editing gear in trunk.

Hike back to "tent city" with camera gear.

Film more interviews.

Eat trail mix and protein shake for dinner.

Hang with Boyd and Christina.

Review the day's work and define the story for tomorrow, the next episode of *Live from "Tent City"*.

Write the voice over.

Turn out the flashlight.

Say my prayers.

Be grateful.

Sleep.

~

But when I get back to "tent city," tonight is different.
Instead of the imagined routine in my mind, reality surprises me.

~

I barely shed my backpack and tripod when a gray pickup and a dark blue sedan pulls up the levee just yards past my tent.

Boyd is already walking up the levee toward the vehicles.

A stocky, young man with black hair and beard pops out of the pickup and waves.

"Hey, Boyd. We brought Sunday dinner for forty."

Six young men and women, maybe 18 to 30 in age, plus one infant, have come to serve dinner in "tent city."

The six turn out to be a local youth group who "received a vision" to feed people in "tent city," so they pooled their resources and raided their pantry shelves and created a giant pot of chili, a huge bowl of salad with assorted dressings, bread, plates, napkins, and forks.

A lean, muscled teen puts the tailgate of the pickup down, and it becomes the buffet counter.

A slight and slender brunette sets a large stew pot of chili on the tailgate.

A smiling, pudgy blonde has her arms cradled around an overflowing basket of bread.

A lanky red-haired lad in glasses is dwarfed by the enormous bowl of salad he carries to the tailgate of the truck.

A young dark-haired mother has an infant in matching bonnet and briefs in one arm and ladles and salad tongs in the other.

Their compassion turns the wasteland from worry into smiles.

These young people put down their video games and left the comfort of a family dinner to create a menu, assemble ingredients, and cook the food now being served with love and smiles, dishing out plates of chili, bread, and salad. These young people found a way to help their neighbors.

A line of hungry "tent city" residents forms quickly down the levee.

In a show of gentlemanly respect, Boyd ushers the women to the head of the line in front of the men so they are served first.

Boyd's authority and manners are unilaterally accepted and observed.

Dinner is now being served at the wasteland.

Everyone is grateful for a hot meal.

"Look. More."

Arms point.

Heads turn.

I pan the camera.

In the distance across the tracks through a cloud of red dust, a caravan of vehicles brings more food and smiles.

It all looks so wonderfully dramatic in my lens – the magic hour's low sun creates a perfect orange backlight, and the caravan in the dust cloud glows in rosy hues.

My telephoto lens magnifies and intensifies the rolling caravan in close-up. Vans and SUV's, wheels churning like eight charging chariots led by a gleaming pearl white Escalade, produce an army of God's angels charging out of the orange cloud of roiling dust.

In bold defiance of the No Trespassing signs, the vehicles roll over the tracks, turning right and set up to feed another part of "tent city," the area closer to the electric substation.

The caravan is here on a mission to care for the poor.

They will not be stopped by No Trespassing signs.

Such random acts of kindness instantly soften the angry hearts and fan the rapidly fading embers of hope.

People blossom with love.

Even homeless people.

The lights in their eyes turn on.

They can feel the caring, and it feels good.

Love heals broken spirits.

Love lifts the downtrodden.

Helping others is a win-win-situation.

And the giver receives the greatest gift of all.

A human soul touched by love rises from the ash heap – a newborn phoenix aglow in the radiance of hope.

For a moment, the light seems to have overtaken the despair.

All is well and happy in "tent city" on this Sunday night because a few people cared enough to make dinner.

One small victory for the light in a sea of desolation.

~

I film an interview with Jimmy Muntreau, a young, muscled church teen in a white cut-off T-shirt.

"Before I came out here and started serving dinners, I thought of the homeless the way everybody else thinks of them. They're lazy. They don't want to work. They are all drug addicts or alcoholics. Yes, those kinds of people may be out here. But there are also people here who want to work, so you have all kinds of people. When I started coming out here, I discovered that everyone is different, and you never get to know who someone is if you judge them first."

~

Don't you just love the wisdom of teenagers, their young minds filled with idealism, altruism, and love?

Take me back to the '60's, Jimmy.

Make love, not war.

I can dig it!

~

All kidding aside, if we ponder the possibility of a coordinated effort among local churches to feed dinner to homeless people in tent cities all across America, Discovery John's vision of a privately-funded Safe Ground begins to manifest before our eyes.

If a lot of people care just a little bit, the caring all adds up to a whole lot of caring, which goes a long way towards helping the needy.

Safe Ground keeps them off the dangerous streets with a safe place to stay, where they won't be sleeping on bus stop benches, and have their very own place to call home.

Imagine that.

Then imagine the reality that if the city fathers evicted one church group who delivered port-a-johns, what will they do to churches who bring food without health permits?

~

You can't feed those people! You don't have a license!

~

What a depressing realization! The city fathers want to rid themselves of the homeless by making homelessness illegal. *And* make laws to fine anyone who comes to help the homeless and the poor.

Is that what our founding fathers said when they arrived in America, homeless themselves after being ejected from Europe?

What about those inscriptions on the base of the Statue of Liberty?

Don't they mean anything anymore?

What up wit dat, America?

What would have happened to our pilgrim forefathers if the native peoples had not helped them that winter by teaching them what to grow, how to plant, and how to shelter themselves against the winter?

It is human nature to help one another.

Who would ever make a law that refuses help to our needy?

Screw that! I refuse to get eaten up by negative thoughts.

No more of the political doublespeak crap in my mind.

It gives me a headache.

I'm going to focus on the human kindness and generosity right in front of me here in "tent city."

That's what I'm gonna do.

~

I head up the levee, gear on my shoulder, to find another angle on the dinner action.

"What da fuck you doin'? You bettah not be filmin' me!"

By the slur, it sounds like this angry man has been drinking.

"Oh, no, it's okay, brother, I got the lens cap on right now. I don't film…"

"Don't be calling me brotha. You ain't my fuckin' brotha. I fuckin' kill ya you be filmin' me, mothafucka. You ain't my brotha!"

Out of nowhere, Boyd imposes himself between me and the angry man, speaking calmly to the man while motioning me with his eyes to move on. He's got it handled.

Boyd takes control of the situation, redirects the angry man's focus to a plate of hot food and guides him back toward his camp without further outburst.

What a comfort to have Boyd as my guardian.

~

I finish writing my voice over for tomorrow's piece.

It's going to focus on Jimmy, a young "normal" guy speaking from "tent city" with firsthand experience of meeting homeless people face-to-face, and how he lived to tell about it!

I keep trying to make light of this situation and laugh 'cause I mainly feel like crying most of the time.

Too much human suffering and sadness to take in 24/7 for this sensitive soul.

I put away my pad and pen and click off my flashlight.

Time for sleep.

"So, Costa, what do you think after your first week in "tent city?" Boyd asks through the tents.

"What week? It's only been five days since I moved in."

We have a good laugh.

I've grown to love the sound of his hearty chuckle.

"Wise ass," Boyd howls.

We laugh again, talking tent-to-tent in the dark. On the wasteland.

"What do I think? I think I am eternally grateful Sister Libby made you my guardian."

"When Sister Libby says do it, I do it."

"Yes, you do!"

"Yeah, so, what do you think?"

"I think it's been pretty amazing, like tonight with the churches catering dinner with dignity and love. How great is that? I love their goodness in the face of darkness shit. That's good story stuff."

"This time of evening is always the toughest for me."

"What do you mean?"

"Every evening after dinner, my dad and I used to sit and talk politics or current events for hours. I haven't spoken to him in six months since our falling out. That sucks. He's so smart, and I always felt like I learned something from him. I miss sitting and talking with him after dinner."

"That's gotta be tough."

"Yeah."

"Hey, thanks for taking care of that guy at dinner."

"What guy?"

"The one that wasn't my *fuckin' brotha…*"

"Oh, yeah, him. That was nothing. One time, I had six guys come at me all at once down at the park. I took every single one of them down. Sent some of them to the ER. I was the last man standing."

"I believe that."

"I'm glad you're here, man. Now, I have someone intelligent to talk to in the evenings. My dad is very smart. He always reads a lot. Newspapers every day. Books. Biographies. I loved those after-dinner talks."

"Do you read a lot?"

"Me. No. I watch people a lot. Everything I learned I got from listening to my dad."

"You get to see a lot of people every day down at the park."

"Eight hundred to a thousand. All kinds of people and all kinds of stories. And would you believe, I hug every one of them who comes to the day shed? That's my mission. Give each person a hug and let them know someone cares. Makes all the difference in the world."

"You are one awesome human being, Boyd Zimmermann."

"It's not me. It's God. I've screwed up my whole life. I'm adopted. I don't even know my birth parents. My adoptive mom and dad have been great. But they didn't like Christina, and they wanted me to disown her. I love her, and I wasn't about to do that just so I could have their money. So, we came here looking for work. This is where I grew up. But there's no work here. We lost everything, but we've worked hard to make a comfortable place for ourselves and tents for our friends. Now, they're pushing us out. Everything happens for a reason, they say."

"You can say that again. Like how Sister Libby assigned you to me. I have no idea anymore. It's all up to God."

"Yeah. Thank God, you didn't turn out to be an asshole after all. You do what you say, and you show respect. That means a lot in my book."

"Thank you."

"And now I got an old man to talk to in the evenings."

Boyd chuckles.

We laugh together. We are quickly becoming friends.

"Good night, son."

"Good night, papa."

"Good night, John boy," Christina joins in.

We go to sleep with happy hearts in the dark.

Six days and five nights in the same clothes.

It got so cold again last night, I could see my breath.

My stream of morning piss makes wispy clouds in the frosted field grass.

I crawl back into the bag and keep my hat on, pulling it down over my head as far as it will go, curling into the fetal position inside my sleeping bag cocoon.

I am happy to report that after six days and five nights in the same clothes, I still smell okay. Or maybe, I'm just getting used to it!

Most of the homeless men in Times Square gave off a strong urine odor that would pierce my nostrils with a pungent ammonia smell.

I don't smell anything like they did.

But I certainly *feel* what it's like being down and out, dirty and cold.

I'm living it just like every other person here in "tent city".

Shortly after I get warm, the Union Pacific comes screeching through "tent city."

I am not quite asleep so I peak out of my tent to see sparks shooting from the wheels of the shrieking steel monster.

When the engineer pumps the brakes, each pump shoots hot iron sparks spraying orange flashes streaking into the steely black night.

I flip my phone open to see the time in the darkness of my tent. 5:12am.

I hear Boyd and Christina heading to work at Friendship Park.

What troopers! I don't know how they have been doing this for eight months, especially Christina with her diabetes and arthritis. She hikes with a cane. Boyd says he's hoping to get her an electric scooter that's being donated to Loaves. She could ride to and from Loaves and alleviate some of the pain of walking.

From what Boyd tells me, he wasn't always this compassionate.

He's been a tough guy most of his life, and many times he's used his height and bulk to get his way, whether by threats or physical violence. Off camera, he shows me gun holes and knife scars on his body and has something like 128 stitches to date so far.

Now, he says he's learned his lessons and is changing himself into a compassionate man. He provides and cares for his woman, Christina. He offers tents, shelter, and community to others and does his best to serve everyone and be a good Christian.

He's just trying to be a good guy for once in his life.

~

I still can't fathom how they've lived like this for eight months, not having a place to take a dump in the morning.

~

Don't get me wrong, Friendship Park provides so much comfort for so many disenfranchised people, but the men's room is rough.

The bathrooms take a real beating.

They are cleaned and hosed down every day, but I'm finicky about where I sit my butt.

I prefer having my own toilet that I don't have to share with anyone else. I don't like to use public toilets for my morning business.

I like the comfort, cleanliness, and privacy of my own personal toilet. Maybe you can relate.

But privacy is not an option when you're homeless.

It's my sixth day using the facilities at the park, you'd think I'd be cool with it.

I'm not.

I don't like having to wipe down a beaten and worn toilet seat before I sit down.

I don't like wondering who was sitting on it before me.

I don't like sitting in a stall with grunting, farting, shitting, and talking going on in the stalls on either side of me.

I just don't feel comfortable or relaxed.

I like to take my morning dump in privacy.

So much for what I want. Ha!

Privacy, comfort, and relaxation while you're taking your morning dump are not options when you're homeless.

The bathrooms at Friendship Park are a morning meeting place, a social hub in a world without running water and sanitation.

Like the village well in olden days, everyone comes to the well sooner or later.

In a simple, basic, and primary way, "tent city" is providing a place where people can feel comfortable because they know their neighbors and have a sense of community.

You can leave personal belongings in "tent city."

I do.

I leave my tent, sleeping bag, suitcase, clothes, flashlight, and toilet kit every day when I hike to Loaves, and it's all there every afternoon when I come back. Of course, being camped next to Boyd adds additional peace of mind.

People are watching out for each other, providing comfort and security and making life a whole lot easier not having to carry *everything around all the time.*

The homeless are never able to relax or let their guard down when they don't have the security of shelter.

It's stressful living on the street, under a bridge, behind a dumpster, in a doorway.

They might get rousted by the police or beaten by thugs in their sleep.

That's why folks who live in "tent city" are getting more anxious with each passing moment. You're more vulnerable on the street. At least here, they felt safe.

Eviction is at hand.

No more neighbors.

No more comfort.

No more community.

Move every day.

Dodge the cops.

No more "tent city."

Here comes "stress city."

~

6:08am is what my phone says.

The sun won't be up for a half hour or so, but the dawn sky fills my tent with soft morning light. It's time for me to get to work.

It's so cold this morning, I can see my breath inside the tent.

I dress quickly and layer-up, adding jeans on top of my long-johns, fleece vest, flannel shirt, turtleneck, and t-shirt above.

I wish I had a fur hat, but my ball cap will have to do for now.

Dressed to fight the morning chill, I get to work.

The first shot I film is from the levee, capturing frost-covered tents at dawn.

I film my voice-overs with this same background, tents shrouded in fog, still in the silver-gray dawn, me telling the story to the camera.

On the other side of the levee, heavy mists cling to the quiet black river.

The beauty of nature contrasts the manmade steel towers, wires, transformers, and the wasteland, now known as "tent city."

"Tent city" is quiet and still in the chilly gray dawn, except for a lone plume of smoke from a morning campfire.

I zoom in for a close-up of a blackened coffee pot percolating on the fire.

By the time I finish the voice-overs, people are coming out of their tents in winter coats and hats, bundled against the morning frost.

When you're homeless, you spend a lot of time out in the elements. You need to dress in layers.

You walk a half-mile to get to breakfast and use the bathrooms, get lunch tickets, shower tickets, and laundry vouchers.

Loaves provides about 100 showers and 100 personal laundries a day.

Only a fraction of the 800 – 1,000 daily guests get to shower or do their laundry on any given day.

It's once a week or every ten days for shower and laundry, is what Boyd said.

~

I finish my filming and pack up for the morning hike to Friendship Park and the bathroom.

I strap on my two backpacks, put my tripod and camera on my shoulder, zip up my tent, and join the flow of homeless headed west to the beckoning mecca of Friendship Park where there is hot coffee, day old cakes, donuts, muffins, and bathrooms.

Sister Libby is amazing.

In her green Friendship Park jacket and cap, she takes the time to stop and say hello to every guest in the Park.

She greets each person with a hug.

Many she knows by name.

Sister Libby touches every heart with her respect and love.

When you get right down to it, what is it that we all want as human beings?

We all want to be loved.

We all want to be recognized.

Sister Libby makes people feel loved and recognized.

She devotes her life to serving and helping others.

When I first met Sister Libby, I thought she treated me special, but I see now this is how she treats every single person she meets each day, with respect, dignity, and compassion.

Sister Libby cares enough about them to stop and share a word of hope and praise and love with them.

She is a living saint.

She lifts heavy hearts, showing each person love and respect, even if only for a moment.

But for that moment in time, one human soul feels worthy and recognized.

Libby sees me and smiles, waves and shouts my name, "Costa!"

~

I have just been publicly blessed by Sister Libby, the patron saint of Friendship Park.

I have received her holy hand of grace for all in Friendship Park to see and behold.

Sister Libby just awarded me the Sister Libby Good Housekeeping Seal of Approval. Maybe now people here in the park and the wasteland won't feel so threatened by me and my camera.

Maybe.

One can always hope.

~

People here in the Park are getting used to seeing me with my camera on my shoulder - or perhaps Sister Libby's public blessing has an immediate impact.

At any rate, the usually suspicious eyes of Friendship Park feel a little friendlier today.

Thank you, Sister Libby!

~

Today, I'm cutting a piece featuring young Jimmy from the youth ministry who came to serve dinner in "tent city" last night.

By 9:00am, I have everything logged and captured.

By the time Boyd shows up on his break around 10:30am, I have a rough assembly which runs about six-and-a-half minutes, twice what I'm aiming for.

Right after Boyd enters, there is a knock at the door.

We can see through the little window in the door that it's Discovery John.

Boyd lets John in. Boyd likes me to keep the door locked for security purposes.

"You never know when some schizophrenic is gonna lose it 'cause they didn't take their meds. You don't need to leave yourself vulnerable to that."

He's always watching out for me. What a guy!

"Looks like they're closing the park tomorrow."

"Why? What do you mean?" I ask.

"Disrespect of the rules. There have been too many violations of the rules lately. On Friday, we caught a couple of guys selling drugs in one of the gazebos. We have a staff meeting coming up before lunch but Garren said it sounds like the perpetrators will be eighty-sixed from the park for a month, and we'll close the park, too, to send a message to all the guests that this behavior will not be tolerated."

"Wow. Is this unusual or what?"

"Probably three to six times a year, we have to shut down the park because of disrespect for the park rules."

John shares his observations.

"They're just dumb. I know those guys. They get their disability checks on the first of each month and like good enterprising businessmen, they pool their resources and buy a pound of weed, so they can sell it and triple their investment. But to sell it in the park? That is just plain stupid!"

"How long will you close the park?"

"That all depends on the severity of the violations. I guess I'll find out at the meeting before lunch. Keep this all under your hat, though. We don't need to start any rumors and get people even more stirred up. Everybody's already on edge about the wasteland shutting down, and there's plenty of rumors about that. Don't need another one. That'd just be fannin' the flames. They'll know soon enough. Keep it quiet for now. I'll let you know when it's okay to talk about it."

"Yes, sir."

"Would you stop that? I told you to stop calling me sir. My dad is sir. Okay?"

"Yes, sir. You got it, brother."

Boyd pretends like he's going to punch the life out of me.

"How do you think he'd look, John, floating face down in the American River?"

"Clothed or naked?" John quips.

"Huh. I hadn't thought about that. Good point. I'll have to think about that."

Boyd chuckles his hearty chuckle.

We all share a moment of levity while we wait for the bomb to drop about the park closing.

~

That means 800 – 1,000 people will have nowhere to go tomorrow.
It's supposed to rain.
Where will they go?
Under a bridge?
In a doorway somewhere?

~

"I gotta get back to work."

"But you didn't get to see the rough cut."

"John can see it. I'll have to see it later. Lock this door behind me."

Boyd lets himself out. I lock the door behind him.

"Well, this is exciting. It's not every day in Friendship Park I get to watch a video in the office next to Nurse Susie."

John has a special flair for the dramatic.

"The honor is all mine. I've assembled most of the shots I want to use to tell the story, but they could be shortened or moved around, so it's a rough assembly. You probably know all this stuff."

"Got it."

I roll the reel.

John watches quietly with focused interest on every shot and doesn't say a word until it's over.

"Well, that's a very interesting perspective, hearing about homelessness from the innocent church youth, but it's too long, and the shots should be shorter. You're playing to an MTV audience and they like short shots and lots of them."

"Very observant, John. Yes, I'm hoping that a young face with a fresh perspective will help shift the way people look at homelessness."

"That's a tall order."

"Yeah. That's the thing with documentaries. You don't get to write and script what happens. You just hope you're ready with your camera when it does happen. It's kinda like sitting at a stakeout. You don't know what's gonna happen or when it's gonna happen; you just know something's going to happen, and you have to be ready when it does."

"Sounds like being homeless to me. We never knows what's going to happen next."

"Right. You don't know if a church is going to show up to feed you, or a cop is going to show up to arrest you."

"It doesn't make any sense. When did it become a crime to be homeless? I lost my job. I didn't rob anyone or steal anything. I lost my home. I didn't kill someone. I have no home. Why is that a crime? What am I supposed to do? Where am I supposed to go? Am I supposed to become invisible? That's how it feels. No one wants to see me. *Be invisible and stay out of my way* is the message they're sending. I would love to oblige them if I only had a place to go."

"I'm hoping these videos will help you get Safe Ground."

"That would be nice."

"Yes, it would."

"Well, I've got to get ready for lunch. Thank you for letting me watch. We're glad you're here."

"You're welcome. I'm glad I'm here, too. Thanks for your feedback."

"MTV. Shorter shots and more of them. The music video generation has a short attention span. See ya."

How refreshing to have communication with an audience even if it is only one person. In theater, you have a live audience, and you know right away if your joke is funny or not. In film, you make the movie in some far away location – like exotic "tent city" – and it's viewed by people you've never met halfway around the world that you never talk to.

As a filmmaker, it's incredibly easy to become obsessive and subjective about my material.

I see that already.

My heart is aching with all the suffering and pain I see.

Why can't I just wave a magic wand and end the suffering?

~

Why is it illegal to shelter yourself on public land?

What are you supposed to do when you lose your job and home?

Why do we spend tax dollars harassing people instead of helping them?

I'm perplexed.

~

Those of us who are fortunate enough to have a home take living inside for granted.

You enter a room and flick a switch, and there is light.

Not when you're homeless.

No home, no electricity, no switch to throw.

When you have a home, you go to the kitchen if you're hungry and open the refrigerator and fix yourself something to eat.

Can't do that when you're homeless.

No kitchen, no refrigerator.

If you're lucky, you got a doggy bag at Loaves.

When it's time to clean up after dinner, you go to the sink and run the water so it's just hot enough for washing and rinsing the dishes. Or maybe you stick them in a dishwasher.

No sink or running water when you're homeless.

No place to clean up.

Did you ever have the urgent need to go to the bathroom, maybe because you were stuffed or maybe you had diarrhea, and you felt like you were going to explode if you didn't get to a toilet right away?

Ain't no toilets in homelessville.

Not since the city eliminated the port-a-johns.

~

The city is closing down "tent city" on the 13th of this month.

That's the date I heard today.

Everybody's freaked.

I'd better call the governor and the mayor and ask them what they intend to do about the promises they made to the people out here.

Add that to my to-do list.

~

Come to think of it, where am I going to go when the city shuts down "tent city"?

Do I stay and continue filming this human suffering and despair?

How can I afford it?

Afford it or not, how can I desert these people in their time of greatest need when they are about to lose the only home they have, a freakin' beat-up tent on a toxic dump site?

How can I afford *not* to stay?

So where will I stay?

Where will I keep my gear?

Where will I edit and charge batteries?

What about my place in Thousand Oaks?

What about my granddaughters?

What am I going to do?

What's your thinking here, God?

Give me a sign so I know I'm doing what you want.

My videos aren't having much of an effect.

Tell me what you want me to do.

Thanks.

I skip lunch in order to finish today's cut in time.

~

Bam!

It's 3:00pm.

The park is closing.

Finished just in time.

I am out the door and across the street to administration to upload to youtube and email the link to my list of 326 friends and associates for distribution.

~

Gray El Greco skies hang low and heavy for my hike back to my tent.

It's cold.

Looks like rain.

Yippee!

It looks like I'm about to find out just how much fun it is to sing in the rain on the wasteland.

Nothing like walking a mile in another man's shoes.

Few people are visible outside their tents as I crest the tracks. Those who are out are bundled in overcoats, hoodies, blankets, and hats against the threatening skies.

The angry gray of the sky reflects the stress on the ground.

"Tent city" doesn't feel like a community this evening.

It feels like scattered tents tied down in fear, awaiting the approaching dark and impending storm.

The powers of darkness are in control.

Boyd comes out of his tent.

"Hey."

"Hey."

"They're closing the park tomorrow. They told us not to tell anyone till after the park closed to avoid possible outbursts in the park."

"So, people won't know until they show up in the morning?"

"We told everyone who was still around after we locked up the park. Word spreads quick on the street. Everybody knows by now."

"So, that's why everything's so tense tonight."

"Okay. Thanks."

~

It will be one week tomorrow since I've moved into "tent city."

I make an executive decision on the spot that tomorrow's piece will be a "week in review" of what I have observed and learned in my first seven days of being homeless in "tent city."

~

I moved into "tent city" on Wednesday the first of April, and I interviewed Joseph on Dreher Street, *Day One*.

"They got to do something to provide a place that's out of the way for these people."

Day Two, Discovery John talked about Second World conditions and Safe Ground.

Day Three, VJ said, "It's a lack of human dignity."

Reno said, "They're spending a million dollars to build a dog park but can't shelter human beings."

Ranjit said, "Being ignored is the biggest pain."

Day Four, someone said, "50 shelter beds for 300 evicted residents of "tent city."

"I'm not leaving these people until a solution is found," I said.

Day Five, Willy said, "People look down on you when you're out here."

Adam said, "It's time for people to be helping people."

Day Six, church groups came to serve Sunday dinner.

Jimmy said, "There's a lot of people out here who want to work."

Oh, what a week it was!

In another episode, I prayed out loud for a benefactor with a piece of land.

A helping hand
just a piece of land
for our fellow man
Is that too much to ask?

~

I sure hope the second week goes better than the first.

There are a lot of veterans and mentally ill folks out here on the street.

They are human beings just like you and me who need compassion and help.

Why aren't the people of America more concerned about this tragic, unnecessary human suffering?

Ignorance and fear reign, while love and compassion heal.

How could we forget the healing power of love?

Fear.

~

I have always had a deep-seated belief – and still do - that human beings are basically 99% good and help their neighbor. It is our nature to be good, do good, help others.

When I knew I was coming to give the homeless a voice, I imagined in my mind what a powerful impact short videos of human suffering could have, circling the globe via the internet.

My visions of viral videos dancing in my head were followed by a mass outpouring of human concern.

My best thinking believed these videos would reach far and wide and help would come flooding in for displaced refugees in America just like it does for refugees around the world.

People would show up with parcels of land.

Millions would make donations.

If 5,000,000 people donate $5 each that is $25,000,000!

Imagine the Safe Ground villages that could be built with $25,000,000!

That's a bunch of shelter for a whole bunch of people who desperately need it.

That is the vision I had when You called me to give the homeless a voice, God.

Was that your vision, too?

Please give me a sign.

I'm confused and need help.

Thank you.

Amen.

Tuesday, April 7

I love the sound of rain on the roof.

I grew up on a farm in Pennsylvania, and the sound of the rain on the tin roof imprinted my young mind with memories of comfort and peace.

I love everything about the rain, how it makes plants grow, how it makes hilltops green, everything except when it seeps into my tent and makes my sleeping bag and duffel of clothing all wet.

I have nowhere to go to stay dry.

I'm in a tent in Sacramento.

This is all I've got right now.

There is no Plan B.

I flip on the flashlight and find a garbage bag to cover the camera gear.

I can wear wet clothes, but I can't shoot with a wet camera.

The show must go on.

~

Water plus dirt equals MUD.

The hard-packed steel gray clay of the wasteland has turned slick overnight.

Out for my midnight piss, walking on the wet clay is like walking on ice but worse. With each step, the clay steps with me, slippery ooze sucking and clinging to my heels.

The headlamp I bought for night shooting comes in handy to find my way in the damp.

From my childhood days camping I know to search for clumps of grass or rocks to walk on to avoid the soggy clay as much as possible.

I only go down once, catching myself on my knee, hand and elbow in the mud.

It was after I relieved my bladder, that could have been messy with a muddy hand.

If I only had a place to wash up and rinse off.

I don't have a place to wash up so I go to the dumpster in search of a towel, a scrap of carpet, or a piece of cardboard to be a doormat to wipe the clay from my shoes.

Mud in the tent is a very bad idea.

There's no carpet, cardboard, or towel in the dumpster.

My tent came in a box, and I still have the box in the tent.

Voila, I now have a cardboard doormat outside my tent!

I find a piece of plaster lath in the dumpster that is perfect for scraping the mud and clay off my only pair of shoes.

If only I had running water . . .

~

Boyd and Christina do not get up early to go to work.

Just like Boyd said, Friendship Park is closed.

And that means no one here has a place to go for coffee and rolls.

"Tent city" looks like a Hooverville from the depression days, gray and muddy in the morning drizzle.

I do my usual, set up to film and record the voice over narration for today's installment of my video report, "Live from Tent City: Day 7".

Boyd comes out of his mega-tent with a mug of steaming coffee to watch me work.

I look at his steaming mug.

"We've got a little gas stove inside. Want some?" he asks, lifting his mug.

"Thanks."

"Cream and sugar?"

"Black."

What a treat! Hot coffee on the levee. But coffee and camera gear in the rain doesn't sound like such a good idea after all. Can't afford an accident.

"Boyd, brother. Cancel the coffee. I'll get it later. Thank you, though."

"You sure? It's no problem."

"I'm sure. Thanks."

Boyd watches in silent observation as I frame up my camera and record the voice over for the day, the "week in review."

He doesn't say a word but watches me through his streetwise squinted eyes.

As I finish, Boyd breaks his silence.

"When Sister Libby brought you over to the Day Storage shed that first day, I didn't think you'd make it this far."

"Thanks for the vote of confidence."

"Would you not be so sensitive and let me finish?"

I silently zipper my lips and let Boyd talk.

"You impressed me with your integrity and character and your respect for the people out here. They can feel it. I know. I talk to hundreds every day, and they talk to me. I can feel it, too. You care. I am honored Sister Libby assigned me to keep an eye on you."

"Thank you, brother."

Boyd's right, I'm too damn sensitive. I look down to hide my embarrassment.

"I would not have made it through a week without you."

"It's not me. It's God. Just remember that, okay?"

"Yes, sir."

"And would you stop calling me sir before I have to kill you myself?"

We share a good laugh.

How blessed I am to have his respect and watchful caring heart on my side.

God always provides a way - in a lion's den, against giants, parting a sea, or in a wet tent on the wasteland.

~

As I'm packing up the gear getting ready to head to town for my daily work, Ronn, the jovial out-of-work carpenter, is out by the "stoop," the wood pile where the guys gather and talk.

I film an impromptu interview.

"Hey, Ronn, what you gonna do today since the park is closed?"

"It affects everybody, not just me. Nobody can go to breakfast this morning or relax in Friendship Park because two selfish stupid jerks - pardon my French but that's what they are, stupid jerks - sold dope in the park. Two jerks mess it up for a thousand others because they're selfish and dumb-ass stupid."

No rest for the weary, just one more bump on an already bumpy road.

The homeless rely on Loaves and Fishes and Friendship Park for sustenance and life.

Where would they eat without Loaves and Fishes?

Where would they rest without Friendship Park?

Where would they bathe?

Where would they do their laundry?

Where would they find Nurse Susie or Reverend Linda for healthcare and counseling? Where would they see Boyd and get his famous hugs at the Day Storage shed?

The park being closed affects me, too.

It means I don't have a place to charge my batteries and log and capture and digitize my footage and edit today's report.

So that means Plan B, I'll work at the library since the park is closed.

But first, I'm going to treat myself to a clean toilet and breakfast, then work.

No coffee, no breakfast, no bathroom today in "tent city."

Just another day being homeless.

You never know what you're gonna find.

Thank God, I have wheels.

~

The work must go on.

I have to get these stories from "tent city" out to the world.

No compassionate caring human being can look the other way and ignore the toll of human suffering right here at home on the streets of our own country, can they?

Americans are renowned for their generosity, helping people in need and crisis all around the world.

Surely, once every American knows the number of homeless refugees right here in the United States, they will rise up and offer a helping hand to assist their fellow countrymen and women who need support right here at home, won't they?

How could they not?

These folks here on the wasteland are registered voters and taxpaying citizens. Because of mental illness, tragedy, disability, depression, they have no jobs, no homes, no cars and no prospects of work.

Is it right that they should be denied the basic human necessities of shelter, sanitation, and water?

Why do we harass and arrest our mentally ill and veterans?

Is that how we treat the "poor and huddled masses" in America today?

What does that say about the health and state of our blessed Union?

~

I load up my gear and hike with my packs and tripod into Loaves to get my car.

It's been a week since I've showered or shaved or changed clothes, and I'm beginning to look and feel like the people I've come to give a voice to.

I can feel the glaring eyes from passing cars as they stare at me with contempt and fear, anger and hate.

Where does all that fear and hate come from?

~

Driving in the car with the radio off I reflect.

It's a place for me to think.

What profound observations can I make after living in "tent city" for seven days?

The city of Sacramento is about to force 250 people out of their tent homes with no place for them to go.

I feel like an alien who landed on a strange planet filled with hate and fear for veterans and people with mental illness.

How can that be?

I'm in shock.

There is a law against camping to make it illegal for a homeless person to set up a tent. But homelessness is not camping.

I have done both and the only similarity is they both use tents.

Where are people supposed to go when they lose their job and have no place to stay?

I'm in shock how we treat the homeless in this country.

Move along or be arrested?

This is not the America I grew up in.

Where's the compassion?

Where's the love?

Helping one another is our purpose here on the planet.

Isn't it?

The way we treat our homeless is a stark reflection of the moral decay of our souls.

When did we stop caring for our mentally ill?

When did we stop helping veterans with haunting, life altering disabilities?

I'm in shock that the governor and mayor have not returned my phone calls.

Why is it no one returns phone calls anymore?

Where's the respect?

Am I the only person seeing this?

Foreclosures are skyrocketing as families lose homes and are forced to the street.

In Sacramento, they arrest homeless people while spending $1,000,000 on a dog park.

In Flint, Michigan, they are bulldozing 80,000 vacant homes to reduce crime and vandalism.

We bail out the banks while we drive neighbors from their homes.

And drive them from their tents.

I'm dismayed that this is what America has come to.

The world is turned upside down.

Has anyone seen the America I grew up in?

Is anyone still alive out there?

~

What the hell was I thinking picking up and moving into a tent with my movie camera?

God sent me.

What the hell was He thinking?

God, did You really call me or was it just my imagination?

I'm living in a war zone.

~

I haven't told anyone about this.

A certain person I ate breakfast with last Friday, who asked to remain unnamed.

I accepted his terms and got a free breakfast and an earful of unusual and disturbing stories.

I shared my state of shock and disbelief about the general lack of concern about homelessness and mental illness.

Mr. Unidentified said to me, "Don't be naïve, Costa, homelessness is big business. Think about it. What's the biggest business in California?"

"Apple?"

"Ha. Corrections."

"Corrections?"

"Jail. Prison. The slammer. Corrections. Where do these people go when the cops take them away? Jail? Did you know the largest collection of mentally-ill is at the L.A. County Jail? Thirty percent of the jail population are mentally-ill. In jail. Do you know what we pay for incarcerating one person for a year in California? Over fifty thousand a head a year. Do the math. Then add in Volunteers of America, The Salvation Army, The Hope Rescue Missions. Big business."

Big business profiting off the hardships of veterans, mentally ill, and the poor?

Is this what we've come to?

Or has it always been this way, the altruistic George Bailey against the greedy Potter? Ebenezer Scrooge? Gordon Gekko in the movie, "Wall Street," "Greed is good!"?

How could I be so naïve?

~

I feel guilty that I'm eating breakfast while everyone else worries in their wet tents.

Hot egg and cheese, 2 for $3 and a clean bathroom.

A little bit of heaven before I head off to work at the public library.

~

I finish breakfast and drive to the library to edit.

I can't afford a $50 parking ticket, so I find a legal space for free on F Street and hike three blocks with gear on my back and gear under my arm to the Sacramento Public Library on I Street.

I feel like a homeless man carrying my life everywhere I go.

I feel the weight of the constant daily struggle and tears begin to run down my face.

Something has to be done about this abomination of needless human suffering.

~

I work to craft a compelling story that will provoke change.

I craft my impassioned plea to the world.

I plead for compassion.

I plead for reason.

I plead for humanity.

I plead for land.

I plead for love.

I cut a good piece, straight from the heart.

After seven hours of creating, I upload *Live from Tent City: Day 7* to youtube before I pack out of the library.

Please, God, show it to millions of people tonight.

~

The rain has stopped but the gray sky hangs low.

As I cross the tracks, I see Boyd and Christina outside their tent talking with their neighbor, the one who doesn't want to be filmed.

The neighbor walks away as he sees me coming.

Boyd has a big smile.

"Hey, brother."

"Hey, brother."

"We got some good news."

"Great. What?"

"You remember Carlos, the little guy that moved in a few days back?"

"Sure. Of course."

"He got a job."

"Fantastic! Is he here?"

Boyd nods to the right.

"He's over in his tent. I'm sure he'd love to tell you his story."

I have little daylight left for filming.

I go to Carlos' tent immediately.

Carlos is excited and happy to tell me his story.

Dampness and chill hang in the air of the encroaching dusk.

Carlos' clothing is layered, a yellow, hooded slicker over a black hooded sweatshirt, pulled close against the chill around his coal black face and sparkling black eyes.

He cuts a striking figure against the dark receding clouds.

"I was working at Circuit City, and I got laid off. I couldn't pay the rent anymore, and I ended up out here."

"Boyd told me you had some good luck today."

"Uh, yes. I was looking for work, and I found a job as a dishwasher and pretty much start on Friday from two to seven. Not everybody out here comes from a good family. I didn't know my mother and father, but I had a grandfather who taught me everything about keeping a positive attitude and carrying myself with respect."

"Boyd told me you change out of your street clothes into a jacket and tie at the park every day and go looking for work."

"Yes, sir, that's right. My grandfather taught me to always dress for success and practice the Golden Rule. So, I carry my clean clothes and shoes to the park every day and change there while I leave my other stuff with Boyd at Day Storage. I am lucky. I had a good grandfather who raised me and cared for me and taught me to do the right thing."

"That makes all the difference in the world, doesn't it?"

"Yes, it does. I have friends who didn't have anybody who cared for them. But I had someone who cared for me. It makes a very big difference. You can't go out looking for a job and tell someone you're homeless. They look at you like you're some kind of drug addict or alcoholic, but, nah, that isn't true. There's a lot of people out here just like me who had a hitch in their lives and now they're trying to climb back out. I'm gonna make it. This is the first step. Now, the city is coming to kick us out, so that's my next challenge. But I'm gonna make it. This is America."

Simple.

Clear.

Compelling.

True.

Success.

Carlos will definitely have the starring role in tomorrow's story, "Live from Tent City: Day 8".

At that instant, a hole in the heavy sky opens.

Dark gray clouds part, double rainbows arc high above the steel towers over "tent city," from the American River to Discovery Park.

A sign from heaven?

I love the magic of Mother Nature.

Out of the storm comes the light.

I film the rainbows until the hole in the sky closes, and they disappear into the blue-black gray of dusk.

With my tripod and camera on my shoulder, I make my way back to my tent, carefully stepping on vegetation and rocks to avoid slipping and falling on the slick clay mud with my gear. Don't want to get the gear muddy. No way!

~

Boyd is holding court outside their tent with several guys I don't recognize.

I meet Philip and Dennis.

Dennis is very talkative and wants to share some of his stories.

He signs a release.

Darkness is upon us, and I have maybe ten minutes to film before it's too dark.

I set up my tripod, level the ball mount, clip the wireless microphone to Dennis' lapel, and start rolling.

Dennis has a full head of sandy blond hair, flopping across his forehead almost covering his blue eyes. He is missing a few teeth.

I see a lot of people with missing teeth among this community.

It's tough to keep good dental hygiene without running water.

The stress of homelessness ages people in hyper speed.

Dennis lives in his car but gets hassled a lot by the police so he came out to "tent city" to sleep. He met Boyd at the day shed, and they became friends. Boyd invited Dennis to stay and gave him a tent. His disability case with the State is pending, but in the meantime, he is basically jobless, penniless, and homeless, yet still hopeful.

"Dennis, with all these challenges, how do you remain so upbeat? I mean, I can feel your pain, but I still see your smile."

"What am I gonna do? Gettin' angry doesn't make it any better. It is what it is. I make my money canning *(collecting cans to redeem the five-cent deposit)*. I have my medical marijuana card for my spine pain. It helps with the pain, but the cops always hassle me about it when they stop me for sleeping in my car. And if I have a beer, I can't stop at one. I get drunk, pass out, and end up in jail. I think I might be an alcoholic."

"You bet, he's an alcoholic!"

Boyd hurls insults and innuendo at every one of Dennis' remarks, like a big brother tormenting his younger sibling.

They're laughing, and it's all in good fun.

Friendship, even when you're being picked on, feels better than loneliness.

That's the way guys are.

If they're friends, they pick on each other.

Friends lighten the load.

A lot of people are about to lose their friends when the city sweeps the homeless off this toxic dump.

I am not making this up. I'm living it!

This is what is happening today in the capital city of the Golden State in the United States of America.

I just want to scream at the top of my lungs, "Wake up America!"

"These people are veterans and mentally ill, and they need our help!"

Have we become so frozen in fear and greed, we can no longer hear a call for help?

~

115

In my tent, writing by flashlight, I finish my script for tomorrow's piece, put my pad and pen in my attaché, turn off the flashlight, and slide into my sleeping bag.

Maybe, tomorrow, it will be sunny, and I can dry out this wet bag and clothes.

Boyd must have heard the click of my flashlight or saw the change in light.

"You done writing for the night?"

"You got it, brother."

"I knew you were. I didn't want to bother you while you were writing."

"Thanks, man. Not a bother. What's up?"

"Nothin'. Just wanted to talk. At home, I used to sit and talk with my father every night after dinner. I miss that."

"Yeah, I know what you mean. It's so great you and your father got to sit and talk every night."

"My dad loved to read. After dinner, we talked about history, politics, and current events every night. You remind me of talking with my dad."

"Well, that's nice, but you don't remind me of talking with my granddaughters."

Boyd has a robust laugh that makes the earth rumble.

Just two homeless men talking through tents.

This is the healthy side of community.

We feel better when we know our neighbors.

Human beings feel better when we're connected, in community, sharing life with others.

Wednesday, April 8

Today is a new day.

The park is open.

The exodus from "tent city" begins around 6:30am.

People scurry out of their tents and head across the tracks, anxious to get back to their morning routine of breakfast at Friendship Park.

~

Adults get cranky without their coffee.

Closing Friendship Park yesterday, on top of the impending eviction made for more worries, more fear, less peace, less love – and lots of cranky adults!

Between the rain, no park, no coffee, no place to go, nerves are unraveling.

No one here is immune from the fear of the unknown.

If I want my favorite muffin, I'd better get in line first.

If I want to take a shower, I need to get to the park early because there are only 100 showers a day.

That's what you think about when you're homeless in Sacramento.

In America, we take living in a home for granted.

Wake up, shuffle to the toilet, flick a switch, shuffle to the kitchen, turn a faucet, make coffee, blah, blah, blah.

But what if you don't have a home?

What if you sleep in your car or on a piece of cardboard behind a dumpster?

Where would you go to the bathroom?

Where would you make your coffee?

Where would you brush your teeth?

Life is very different without a home.

When we live inside, coffee, convenience, and comfort are expected, a given, taken for granted.

When you're homeless, you have to go to Friendship Park to get coffee and comfort.

There is no convenience when you're homeless.

People start gathering at the gates before 6:00am, even though the park doesn't open till 7:00am.

~

Christina was a carney before her health deteriorated. The carnival midway is a great place to observe human behavior. She always wears an innocent smile, but underneath, she is a savvy observer, measuring each individual, sizing up every situation.

Sleeping in a tent on cold, damp April nights aggravates her joint pain from rheumatoid arthritis. Nevertheless, Christina serves others with a smile, hiding her pain. But when she leaves at the end of her shift, she has to walk with two canes.

Boyd works part-time at the park, manning the Day Storage shed.

The homeless can store up to one bag a day at the shed, which is great if you live on the street. You don't have to carry everything you own with you everywhere you go all day long.

When you have a home, you can leave all your clothes, food, and toothbrush at home.

When you don't have a home, you can't leave anything, you have to keep everything you own with you because if you don't, there's a good chance it won't be there when you return.

Boyd's a big guy, over 6 feet and 300 pounds with a full head of wiry hair and a mangy reddish gray beard.

If you saw him in a dark alley, you would run the other way.

But he does more than just store your gear.

At Friendship Park, he says good morning and gives a hug to every person he serves.

Many of his teeth are rotted and gone, but it never stops him from smiling and laughing and sharing love with every single person who crosses his path.

It's enlightening to witness his compassion in the face of so much adversity.

~

I spend 6–7 hours a day in my "editing room" at Friendship Park.

Boyd pops in regularly to check on my progress, watching in silent amazement as he and friends from "tent city" fill the screen.

I tell him my idea for the story of the day, and he offers his thoughts.

When Sister Libby first introduced me to Boyd, his body language was stiff and guarded.

Now, we're friends and brothers.

"Ya know, when Sister Libby brought you over to me a week ago, I had serious doubts about you and your intentions. But you really surprised me. You've done everything you said you were gonna do and then some. You're a man of your word and that means a lot on the street. On the street, all we've got left is our word. You treat everyone with respect. You're all right in my book."

Respect is good.

The Golden Rule works.

~

Homeless people aren't born homeless.

Every human being deep down inside wants to be respected and to feel that their voice is being heard – homeless or not.

Boyd was a truck driver, John was a contractor, Coyote was a horse trainer, Cowboy Bill was a marine and fought in Viet Nam, Christina ran a game booth for a traveling carnival.

There are contractors, carpenters, roofers, plumbers, electricians, architects, designers, landscapers, tilers, painters, plasterers, masons, and general laborers.

All those jobs are gone.

So how do all those people who no longer have jobs take care of their families and pay their mortgages, healthcare, food, clothing, and education bills?

I don't have a research team to run all the numbers and give you the hard facts but you can do the math yourself – how many millions of American workers lost their jobs when the bottom dropped out of the housing market?

~

It has been one week since I moved into "tent city."

I live among the disabled, mentally-ill, veterans, misfits, and outcasts here.

~

My heart is sick.
My mind is overwhelmed.
What the hell am I supposed to do?

Thursday, April 9th

Carlos owned no sleeping bag, no tent, and had no idea what he was going to do come nightfall, until he talked to Boyd.

Now, he has a tent, a job, and hope.

~

Boyd witnessed the increasing numbers of homeless people on the streets every day, so when the church wagons came around donating sleeping bags and tents, he stockpiled bags and tents, giving them away to people who showed up later, with nothing but the clothes on their backs.

It was Boyd's way of helping those in need, a way to help ease the shock, while the new folks got their bearings in this strange land of "homelessville."

~

In "tent city," I see community, caring, and compassion.

In the suburbs, I see disconnection, isolation, and dysfunction.

We need to ask ourselves if it's okay to treat our veterans and mentally ill this way.

~

My heart cries out for the future of our children and grandchildren.

~

I still get daily threats from angry residents, but Boyd tells me not to worry; he's got my back.

I do my best to appear strong and confident.

I have to hold on to my purpose for being here and stay focused on my mission.

Or I could end up like one of my neighbors.

Homeless.

~

I cut the piece on Carlos' success story by 3:00pm and upload it to youtube before the offices close at Loaves at 5:00pm.

While I'm online, I check the views on Jimmy's piece – 321.

Yay, numbers are up!

Then I check out a video with over 1,000,000 views – a bulldog on a skateboard.

It was cute.

Fun.

But cute and fun are two things homelessness is not!

What do I have to do to get 1,000,000 views for the homeless?

Friday, April 10th

The morning is gray and damp. I'm usually one of the first ones up and out in "tent city" after Boyd and Christina, but the first sound I hear this morning is car wheels rolling over gravel up the levee just above my tent.

A voice calls out, "Railroad police, comin' to town! Railroad police, comin' to town!"

What is going on?

Railroad police?

My mind is racing – *what does that mean, railroad police?*

I quickly build my camera and microphones to get ready to start filming immediately, as I listen to the sounds and shouts through my tent.

Shoes on and camera built, I zip up my tent and carry my gear up the levee. The height gives me an overview so I can assess this morning's presence of police activity.

Out of a big white Lincoln Navigator SUV and a black Chevy Tahoe SUV come two men in dark blue uniforms. I can see through my telephoto lens that they are the Union Pacific Police.

Railroad police.

"Tent city" is bordered on three sides by railroad tracks.

I guess it makes sense that the railroad police would be here. It is their property.

But what is their purpose at 6:21am this gray and misty morning?

I guess they've done their homework and know it's the best time to catch the residents at home.

Most of the "tent city" residents are outside their tents and watching from a distance, gathering and talking "What do the po-po want now?"

The railroad police approach the tents, announcing their police presence, handing out yellow eviction notices and informing residents that they are trespassing on Union Pacific land. They have 72 hours to vacate the property before Union Pacific takes further action to remove them and their belongings.

Most residents stare at the eviction notices in stunned silence, accepting the notice and their fate.

When you're homeless, you have to move when you're told to move, or you go to jail.

Some are silent.

Some weep.

Some scream in anger.

Rio is pissed, waving the yellow notice threateningly above his head.

"What the fuck is this? Where are we supposed to go? There ain't no shelter beds left! Where the fuck are we supposed to go? Fuck that. I'm staying here. Arrest my fuckin' ass. I ain't leavin'. I'm stayin' right here!"

Karen weeps openly, "What am I supposed to do? Where am I supposed to go? This is the only home I have! What's going to happen to my cat? Where am I supposed to live?"

~

If it is our nature as Americans to help others in need, why aren't we helping these people? They're Americans, too.

Is it because they're mentally ill and we don't understand mental illness?

~

Studies have shown that it is more cost-effective to care for the disabled and the mentally ill rather than letting them fall to the streets. Arresting and incarcerating the disabled mentally ill homeless costs nearly three times more than housing and caring for them. Go figure.

So, why is it that instead of housing the disabled, needy, mentally ill and veterans, we arrest and incarcerate them?

Why do we pay for police action and jail when we could house and help for one-third the cost?

Wake up, America, I've got a major news story to break. . .

IT COSTS LESS TO HELP PEOPLE THAN TO JAIL THEM!

The sheer absurdity of it all is making me nuts.

The homeless have been disenfranchised and discarded. Doorways and alleys are littered with homeless who have been labeled with the common public misperception that they are all lazy, drunken drug addicts. We see them as a nuisance and a blight!

This epidemic of homelessness is not going away until we take action to get the mentally ill and veterans housed immediately. That would probably take care of the majority, maybe as much as 75% or more.

The rest can be addressed through caring, compassion, and love.

The solution is clear.

It's time to put down the fear and time to help others.

~

But when you lose everything, then what do you do?

My fellow Americans . . . Our forefathers were homeless!

Your grandparents and great-grandparents traveled thousands of miles from distant lands and arrived off the boat homeless.

~

When I grew up, we started every day in school with the Lord's Prayer and the Pledge of Allegiance. We stood next to our desks in homeroom and prayed and pledged together. We were also taught the Golden Rule. The Ten Commandments hung on a large, wooden plaque outside the principal's office.

At home, when we sat down for dinner, before anyone took a bite, we would bow our heads and pray.

Today it's different.

When was the last time we sat down to dinner with the whole family together?

When was the last time we said the Lord's Prayer?

Call me corny, but when you take God, discipline, and structure out of family, what you get is what we have today.

History shows when we live life without morals, self-discipline, family, and God, we humans tend to make a mess of things. We're real good at trashing things. Just look at what we've done to Mother Earth.

Why don't we help these people instead of harassing and jailing them?

Where are the veterans, disabled, and mentally ill going to go when the "tent city" eviction finally happens?

I'm mad as hell. What am I supposed to do with all this human suffering and ignorance, all this fear and hate?

You called me to give the homeless a voice, but no one wants to listen. No one cares.

What am I supposed to do?

~

Carved into the base of the Statue of Liberty is a poem by Emma Lazarus, an immigrant from the late 1800's. "Give me your tired, your poor, your huddled masses, yearning to breathe free... Send these, the homeless, tempest-tost to me, I lift my lamp beside the golden door!"

When did it become a crime to be poor and homeless in America?

Fear.

Anxiety.

Stress.

The railroad police just jacked 'em through the roof!

Everyone's being evicted.

Where are they going to go?

Where am I going to go?

~

In a fit of adrenalin, I go online and check the number of views on my first week of youtube posts I call *Live from Tent City*.

Bad idea. My heart crashes through the floor. I was hoping that by now at least one of my posts would have a thousand views. How naïve of me to think people would actually be interested in seeing and helping the homeless.

Sorry to sound so cynical. I'm just discouraged.

~

Did you ever travel somewhere with luggage – an airport, a train station, or a bus depot? Do you remember how you felt after an hour of walking and hauling your luggage everywhere you went?

Now imagine if you did that 24/7, every hour of every day while strangers and passersby looked at you with contempt and derision, and the police harassed and arrested you?

And when you had to go to the bathroom, all the public restrooms are locked?

And you're still pulling all your luggage behind you everywhere you go?

Now imagine doing all this while you've got the flu or your leg's in a cast.

Many of the homeless are sick or disabled. If you're disabled in an airport, there are porters and motorized carts to help you out.

Can you imagine maneuvering luggage being in a wheelchair or on crutches without help?

That's what it's like to be homeless in America.

Did you know that nearly 50% of the homeless population suffers some form of mental illness? And over 25% of homeless people on the streets are veterans?

~

I'm beginning to think that the homeless problem is predominantly a mental health problem. Mental illness is a tough one for us Americans.

With a skinned knee, a chipped tooth, or a broken wrist, we can see the injury.

With mental illness, the injury is invisible.

There's no scratch, no bruise, no runny nose.

"You don't look sick to me."

If we can't see the signs of sickness, you must not be sick.

So, we look the other way without understanding the problem or providing treatment.

And that's how our mentally ill end up on the street.

I'm not a doctor or a scientist, a psychiatrist or a politician, but from what I've seen, our current policies do not seem to be the most effective way to handle and treat mental illness.

The system is broken.

Mental illness will not be fixed by looking the other way.

~

I am so mad at the indifference I see on youtube, I call the mayor's office again to see if I can get an interview.

The mayor isn't in, so I leave another message.

Then I call the governor's office again.

The governor isn't in, either, so I leave another message there, too.

Surely these people, these heads of city and state, these elected officials have a plan for what they intend to do with the 300 people being evicted. They wouldn't just evict 300 disabled homeless people without a place for them to go. Right?

From where I'm sitting in my tent, I am beginning to have serious doubts about the vision of our leadership in America today.

In business, arts, and entertainment, America is thriving. Silicon Valley is the new center of forward-thinking creativity for the world. Americans are bold, not afraid to take risks or strike out into the unknown. Microsoft, Apple, Tesla, Google, Facebook continue to dazzle consumers and thrive in the midst of an international widespread recession and economic collapse.

Why are our government, judicial system, law enforcement, mental health, healthcare, infrastructure, and education failing us?

Imagine if a Silicon Valley brain trust focused on fixing America's mistakes!

I'd like to see that.

~

I hope I didn't see what I just saw.

I just saw a woman wrapped in a sleeping bag in the gray morning mist of "tent city" eating out of a dog food can.

~

Here I am in the greatest country in the world – or at least it was when I was growing up – surrounded by prosperity and abundance, but our leaders don't have a plan to address the needs of mentally and physically disabled citizens and veterans.

How can that be?

Life is upside down.

We spend money for a dog park, but we don't help our mentally ill.

Upside down.

Fear is rampant.

Where did all the love go?

Upside down.

~

"People are getting scared. Where are they gonna go?" Boyd voices the energy of the tense morning.

"Everybody has no place to go." Christina's voice wavers with tears in her throat.

I feel so helpless.

I came here to give these people a voice, but no one wants to hear them.

What am I supposed to do?

All I can do is keep filming, stay focused on my "mission," and trust that God knows what He is doing calling me here.

Trust isn't easy for me when I am overwhelmed by the emotion of human suffering all around me. In the face of all this illogical suffering and indifference, I feel as if my efforts are falling short.

I'm letting the homeless down.

I'm letting God down.

I'm a failure.

~

According to John, Batman and Robin (the nicknames for the cops who run the homeless beat) told him that the city's attitude towards homelessness is that "if you're nice to poor people (homeless, disabled, mentally ill) and make it easy for them, then everyone will want to be homeless, and people will come from all across America to be homeless in Sacramento."

Really?

If those same politicians came out and lived in "tent city" for just one week with no toilets, no running water, no electricity, no privacy, they might have a different opinion about how appealing it is to be homeless in Sacramento. Or anywhere.

The world is upside down.

The physically disabled, with broken arms, gimpy legs, and injured backs are on the streets. How much healing is going to happen on the street?

Veterans who can't adjust from the killing life to the "normal" life are on the streets.

The mentally ill, depressed, bipolar, and schizophrenic are on the streets.

Now add all the people from the economic crash, on the street.

And all our politicians can do is bail out the banks!

Stop and think about the domino effect that happens when an economy stops building.

Don't need carpenters. Don't need plumbers. Don't need electricians, masons, sheet-rockers, plasterers, tilers, HVAC, contractors, architects, surveyors, inspectors, laborers, nothin'!

And that all adds up to fewer taxes collected by cities.

So cities have to cut costs, downsize, and lay off government workers.

The dominoes continue to fall.

Every one of the homeless at one time or other worked a job, had a family, a home, and a life.

These people are not lazy. They are in shock, trauma, and disbelief.

And now their lives are upside down.

The solution in Sacramento is to write laws to prohibit people from putting up a tent, remove benches from bus stops, lock up all the public toilets, write laws to make it illegal to feed the poor and hungry, and hire more police to keep the homeless moving.

Our forefathers would be rolling over in their graves if they knew that over 25% of the homeless people on the streets are veterans.

Everything's upside down.

Women eating dog food.

Families without shelter.

Veterans needing mental health care.

What ever happened to this sweet land of liberty?

America the beautiful isn't looking so beautiful anymore.

I used to be proud to be an American.

Now, I am ashamed.

If we keep living our lives driven by hate and fear, we will continue to wallow in paranoia and bitterness, instead of light and love.

~

I was fortunate to grow up in a home which valued God, helping others, and living every day with honesty and integrity. Now, I do my best to set the same example for my children and grandchildren. How could I tell them to help others if I didn't help others first?

~

Indulge me for a second, please and take a walk with me in these homeless shoes.

If you lost your job and couldn't make your house or rent payments, what would happen to you and your family?

Now if after six months, you still didn't have work and couldn't make your car payments and your insurance payments, what do you think would happen to you and your wife and kids?

You would not have a home anymore. The bank owns it. You would be foreclosed.

You would not have a car. The bank owns it. It would be repossessed

Without a home and a car, how are you going to find a job and feed your family?

Now what do you do?

A moment ago, you were a "normal" American - working a job, paying your bills, living on credit, and buried in debt. Now, you're on the street, nowhere to go and the "normal" people are looking at you with contempt and hate - and you're still buried in debt.

Would *you* want to live in a tent?

Sometimes when we take a walk in another person's shoes, life looks different from our original preconceptions.

~

The spiritual teachings from thousands of years ago still hold true today.

Judge not, lest ye be judged.

There but for the grace of God go I.

In a nutshell, that's the truth.

~

Do we really think if we hide our heads in the sand, homelessness will all go away?

We tried that before. It was called the Dark Ages. They were dark ages because the human spirit was dark, filled with fear, greed and selfishness, every man for himself.

Sounds familiar, doesn't it?

But we must ask ourselves, is fear, selfishness, and greed really the best way to live a healthy, happy, purposeful life?

We live in the land of the free.

Our choices are our own.

Is fear the answer?

Or is it love?

What do you choose?

~

"Tent city" is quiet tonight in spite of the high level of anxiety.

Around midnight, I am awakened by a loud, angry voice outside my tent.

I'm startled, scared, and wondering if this is an impending threat on my life that friends warned me about.

I can see the headlines, "Filmmaker Murdered in Tent."

I grab my tripod in case I have to defend myself. It has steel points at the tips.

But it's just old Tom, who's had too much to drink.

Boyd reacts immediately in a loud voice. "Quiet, Tom, everybody's sleeping."

I can hear the tent flaps rustle as Boyd exits his tent and strides across the gravel to speak to Tom in a low voice. Boyd has the situation quietly handled in under a minute.

Boyd is a good neighbor with a helping hand. He watches out for all his friends.

The freight rolls through at 2:07am. Tonight the train rumbles through with a hypnotic rhythmic beat – ke-dunk-ee-dunk, ke-dunk-ee-dunk, ke-dunk-ee-dunk – the wheels on the tracks like a giant, alien cricket chirping its mating call, no shrieks, no sparks.

I think it must be a different brakeman.

On the noisy nights, it was an angry brakeman who doesn't like the "lazy, drunk homeless people," so he hits his brakes to jar the "bums" from their sleep.

On the quiet nights like tonight, the brakeman must not hate the homeless so much.

Why do we have so much hate for humans down on their luck?

It hit me like a ton of bricks.

Is this our greatest fear
that we will end up homeless,
just like them?

Do we loathe them because we, ourselves are only a paycheck away from being them, another bag lady, another "worthless bum," trying to survive on the ugly streets of hate?

The labels we heard growing up are buried deep inside until we must face homelessness ourselves.

That is a frightening thought! Me, homeless?

Instead of having compassion and understanding, fear grabs us by the throat, and we run the other way, but the sick feeling inside us never leaves. The fear lingers and simmers deep in our souls. Maybe, that's the whole problem in a nutshell.

When our souls are sick and *dis-eased*, we react and push the ugly away, repress it, deny it, and blame it on others like those "lousy, lazy filthy bums" over there.

But blaming others never fixes fear because fear lives inside us.

Fear, like happiness, is an inside deal.

It's a choice.

We get to choose fear or choose love in every situation we face.

We can blame others all we want, but the problem remains ours.

The problem is within.

Fear is ugly.

Love is good.

Which one are you choosing to live your life?

We must go inside to make the choice.

~

Jim Peth has been a director at Friendship Park for 17 years. He left his career as a high school teacher/coach because he had a calling to serve the poor and the homeless. He readily signs a release and happily takes time to share his experiences with me.

"Jim, you've seen a lot over seventeen years here. Why do people become homeless?"

"Why do people become homeless? That's a good question, and there isn't just one pat answer. Every person is different and how they got here is different. From what I've seen, one thing that many or most have in common is a high percentage of our folks experienced some degree of neglect or abuse at an early age."

"We had one gentleman here who told me that he left home at the age of 9. Now, you have to ask yourself, what was going on at home that a 9-year-old boy would feel safer living on the streets than being at home?"

"We come into the world as babies, unable to take care of ourselves, relying on the care of others to feed us, bathe us, and love us. We are totally dependent on our parents for everything and that is where we learn how to cope and move forward in life."

"What do you think was going on in that house that a 9-year-old boy felt safer on the streets? Was there caring? Was there guidance? Did someone read to him every night before bed? Probably not. Psychologists say that up to 95% of imprinting of the human mind takes place from birth to five years old. So, you have to ask yourself, what was the imprint on this boy in the first five years? Did he learn to read? Did he learn math? Did he learn the warmth of family? Did he learn love? Probably not, no one read to him, and no one loved him. Now put that same boy on the street at nine years old, and he will have a pre-conceived notion that life is rough and everyone is out to hurt him."

"It all begins at home. Was home a warm, nurturing, loving, fun place? Or was there no family dinner, no family play time, and no family love time? At home, we create a blueprint of love and nurturing, or we create a blueprint of neglect and need. Human beings thrive on love. Without love, we are lost. We feel unloved, not worthy and are often times angry because we didn't get loved at home. What's the old saying, the apple doesn't fall far from the tree? Neglect and abuse are very unhealthy for humans."

"Jim, one of the things that struck me the first time I saw "tent city" was the sense of community. People were watching out for each other. Why do you think that is?"

"I think it's because they didn't have a sense of community at home. They are trying to create that comfort and caring for themselves in "tent city" because they never got it at home. Some of us spend our whole lives searching for the attention and love we never got at home."

"Jim, eviction from "tent city" seems like it could happen any day now. What will the fallout look like?"

"There are going to be a lot of angry people with the evictions. We are already seeing tempers flaring and more fights in the Park. Everyone is feeling more stressed out every day. It's a ticking time bomb about to blow. All we can do here at Friendship Park is provide a little food, a bathroom, a place to rest for a few hours, and love."

~

Under constant stress, the mind spirals downward and begins to expect the worse.

Are they coming today?

Will the police and trucks and bulldozers roll up today?

Where will three hundred disabled, mentally ill go?

Will Mayor Kevin Johnson return my phone call and grant an interview?

Will Governor Arnold Schwarzenegger return my call today?

Is there anyone in political power who has the courage and compassion to act like a leader and be accountable to his constituency?

Or is public fear that much louder than love?

Get those "lazy bums" out of here! yells the constituency.

~

I hope I'm wrong but it looks like fear is in charge.

~

Enut is wearing a Forty-niners jersey and a steel chain across his chest. He is angry as he stomps up to me and my camera.

"Is that thing on?"

"Sure, Enut, what's on your mind?"

"I'll tell you what's on my mind. Where the hell is Oprah? She started this whole thing. Everything was fine before she showed up. Nobody bothered us out here before Oprah. She started this whole thing. She has the money. Why doesn't she come down here and do something about this? So, if you're listening, Oprah, are you going to come down here and help clean up the mess you made? We were fine before you showed up, Oprah. That's all I've got to say."

"Thank you, Enut."

"Damn straight. You think she's gonna see that?"

"I sure hope so. I'm pretty sure she has the internet."

"Damn straight. You right about that."

We do a white brother handshake and hug.

Enut hefts a stuffed, black, 55-gallon bag full of his "stuff" over his shoulder.

"I'm goin' down to the river. Gonna find me my own spot."

He heads out of the park with his life over his shoulder and his trusty pit bull on a leash by his side. Man and dog, friends for life.

I film them as they leave.

~

The energy is wild and frenetic in "tent city".

Everyone has a story to tell today.

~

Do you know what it's like to live in fear every moment of every day?

I guess if you lived in the Middle East you know. Guns going off, bombs exploding, friends and loved ones being killed before your very eyes, homes destroyed, no water, no food, no toilets, no peace.

That's what if feels like here. I am in a war zone. My senses are on high alert at all times. I don't know where my next meal will come from. I don't know where I will sleep tonight, or if I will sleep at all. Is the next person I meet going to say hello or beat me up and rob me blind? Is this policeman here to help me – or hurt me? Can I trust anyone?

This is the state of affairs right now in Sacramento and in cities across America – war.

War against the poor.

War against the mentally ill.

War against the disabled.

War against our very own veterans.

This is America today.

I am witnessing it, filming it, and living it.

War against our own citizens, the poor and the needy.

This is not the America I grew up in.

This is all upside down.

~

A giant wave of uncertainty hangs over the wasteland. The rising tide of eviction cannot be held back. The city is more powerful than the people.

Unless God decides to intervene with angels and trumpets, the exodus is about to begin.

~

"Tent city" was home.

Not anymore.

Roam the streets searching for safety, behind a dumpster, an overgrown hedgerow, a recessed doorway, any place to rest until you are forced to move again.

~

Boyd has been talking with Garren and John, and they have come up with a plan. Boyd shares the plan with me and Christina.

"We're moving tomorrow. Garren thinks if we get away from the railroad right-of-way we might be safer – for a little while longer anyway. We're gonna move up the levee to the radio tower. Garren says we'll be off the Union Pacific land and then it falls back to the city to see what they're gonna do. We'll pack up and move at dawn. That's the plan. Okay?"

"What are our options?" I ask.

"There are no options. That's it. It's either move up the levee or back to the streets."

"And then what? How long until the city comes in?"

"Tomorrow. Next week. Who knows? We'll deal with that when it happens. For now, we're moving up the levee in the morning."

Boyd puts a big bear arm around Christina to comfort her, and they head back to their tent arm in arm.

"Everything's going to be just fine, honey."

Love is alive, even in war.

~

Maybe the mayor will return my call and grant an interview today.

Maybe the governor will call, too.

Then again, maybe not.

Maybe their silence speaks volumes.

Maybe the American ideals are a figment of my imagination.

Why do we deny our homeless veterans, disabled, mentally ill, needy and poor citizens the basics of water, sanitation, shelter, and healthcare?

Let me ask that another way.

Why are we not helping our fellow Americans?

If we stopped to love our fellow man instead of turning away in fear, we could solve this problem immediately.

Why is fear seemingly so much stronger than love?

~

Boyd and John are talking about "Safe Ground" again.

"All we need is a vacant piece of land like the one down on 7th by the old railroad yards. Or the wasteland, right here. Or even an empty warehouse. All we need is a place to wash up, store our gear, a place to call "home" that keeps us off the streets and helps us get our lives back together. Maybe even get a job."

This community is about to be torn apart and destroyed.

"We've been out here eight, no nine months now. It's hard out here. People can fall and never get back up. It's hard on the body and really hard on the mind. Christina's rheumatoid arthritis is debilitating. She sleeps in pain every night and wakes up in pain every morning, because the cold and damp out here mess with her joints. She's not going to heal and get better out here. I need to get her inside. This living outside is gonna kill her."

Boyd is in conflict.

He has devoted the past nine months helping his homeless brothers and sisters with tents, sleeping bags, hugs, and advice. But Christina is suffering, which means if he gets them inside, he would no longer be on the streets helping those in such dire need.

Buried beneath layers of shirts for warmth, I can see Boyd's sensitive heart struggling. It's tearing him up.

"So, we'll pack everything up and move up the levee tomorrow. Maybe that'll give us the break we need. Or at least a few more days until we get run off."

Frustration, confusion, and a sliver of hope, perhaps.

Where are we supposed to go?

Saturday, April 11th

The rain has passed.

The sun is up.

It's moving day in "tent city." It is a beehive of activity, everyone scurrying, sorting, packing, and loading everything they have in their possession and trashing what they don't want.

~

Exodus is a recurring theme in human history.

Refugees are everywhere throughout the history of mankind.

Refugees in Rwanda.

Refugees in Liberia.

Refugees in Europe, Africa, China, Russia, refugees in America.

Ever since Moses led the Jews out of Egypt, there have been refugees.

Even our forefathers who came to America were refugees driven from Europe by religious persecution.

They fled to the "New World" with hopes of freedom and liberty.

Now, we have homeless refugees in every town and city across America.

Boyd and Christina have been here for nine months. Boyd has done everything possible to make it livable and comfortable for them. He created a tent mansion out of three tents fitted together, complete with a bedroom with a queen size box spring and mattress; a sitting room with folding chairs and mini fridge; and a dressing room with a handicap toilet. He even rigged up a series of batteries to chill the fridge and power a TV at night so Christina could watch American Idol.

A noble savage on the trash heap of human suffering.

~

Whether it's 500 yards or 500 miles, moving is moving.

And moving is stressful.

Because everything must move.

But surprisingly, the energy this morning in "tent city" is one of camaraderie and hope. Neighbors are helping each other carry belongings up the levee, bicycles and boxes, rolling carts and black plastic trash bags, stuffed with belongings.

There is the occasional random scream of frustration and flying objects hurled in anger, but overall, people are helping people in the dirt and the dust.

I'm half expecting Moses to show up!

But Moses is a no-show.

It's just me filming a gaggle of misfits walking, dragging, shuffling, pulling, pedaling, rolling, carrying, lugging everything they own to a new spot, with a slimmer of hope for peace.

Bringing up the tail end of this ragtag parade of rejects and outcasts is one big tent floating above the levee. It is being carried by Carlos, Redwood, Pete and Boyd, one at each corner of the tent. They are joking and laughing and one of them starts to sing "Old Man River."

~

Will the move make a difference?

Or will we be evicted anyway?

~

Giddy hopefulness fills the camp, as if the move has temporarily erased the impending doom of eviciton. Tom raises the stars and stripes next to his tent to show his patriotic pride. By late afternoon, Boyd is reconstructing his three tents, tying them all together and staking them down.

~

The land we vacated is now empty, except for a few piles of trash. The wasteland has been returned to its natural state – a dump.

Sunday, April 12th

It's Easter morning.

Resurrection is rebirth, renewal, a second chance, and a reason to celebrate. Yet, my heart is heavy and filled with sadness. I know God called me to give the homeless a voice, but right now, I just want to go home. All I want is to be home with my granddaughters.

What am I doing here?

Nobody watches my "Live from Tent City" reports anyway.

It's the same way people act when they have to deal with a homeless person. No one wants to see the dirty, ragged, mentally ill, disabled, and poor. Most people just look away or move away.

What can I do, they think?

I might get hurt if I try to help.

What can I accomplish anyway?

I'm only one person.

I'm going to church before I become totally cynical and engulfed in anger, resentment and self-doubt.

Hopefully, God will have answers for me.

I prayed. "Father God, Creator and Giver of all life and love, I am here for You. You called me to serve. But I am feeling helpless and inadequate. These people are about to be evicted and thrown out on the streets. I feel like I've failed. How am I supposed to give these people a voice if nobody wants to listen or see? Guide me, God, so I can do Your will. I am weak and need help. Give me a sign. Tell me what you want me to do. Thank You, God. Amen."

~

My favorite part of church is the singing.

There is something about all these voices united together in one song, one purpose, one word that makes me feel like I belong and everything is okay.

For me, it's the power of unity and togetherness, forged into one harmonious vibration of community, a oneness of sound from many voices. I sing through my tears and find comfort in song.

But I don't hear any answers from God about my wavering faith.

How did Paul stay in faith all those years in prison?

How did Daniel remain strong in the lions' den?

How did Shadrach, Meshach, and Abednego stay in faith in the fiery furnace?

They had faith and belief, and they prayed a lot.

I pray a lot but my faith and belief are under assault and shaky.

After ten days in "tent city," I'm ready to turn tail and run home to my family for comfort and love. I'm not sure I can keep the faith much longer.

What kind of wimp am I?

I have a whole lot of questions and so few answers.

~

Church gives me a little hope but not the answers I had hoped for.

I'm too emotional to talk with anyone. I keep my sunglasses on and spend the day to myself, hiding behind my camera, composing wide shots of the new camp and the remains of the old camp from afar while pondering my future, digging myself deeper into my self-made hole of contempt and self-pity.

Maybe it's time to pack up and leave.

~

Tom was a carpenter. One day, he was finishing up a job and a 700-pound toolbox slipped and crashed down on him and broke his spine. His spine had to be fused, and he can't work anymore.

With no money coming in, he fell behind in his mortgage payments, car payments, utilities, cable, phone, credit cards, and wifi. The bank foreclosed on his house and repossessed his car.

Homeless without wheels, he ended up on the street and met some people who told him about "the wasteland." He's been here over a year.

Earnest was a roofer for 30 years.

Here in "tent city" he built sidewalks out of pallets to keep the mud out of his tent, and has a picket fence around his tarp-covered "house," right here in "tent city."

"I was making $1,500 a week! I always had money back then. I would see homeless people every day. Sometimes, I would give them money, and sometimes, I wouldn't, but I never once thought about *being* homeless. Then everything changed. The economy crashed and construction came to a screeching halt. They stopped building houses. They didn't need roofs anymore."

"Thirty years bent over a roof does some serious damage to a back. Who's gonna hire a fifty-year-old dude with a bad back, anyway? Of course, I thought with thirty years of seniority, I would be okay. But no, that wasn't the case. Whatever repair jobs there were, went to family members first."

"I'm divorced. My kids are grown. They live with their mother. I couldn't pay my rent, so I moved back in with my mom, but the neighborhood had gotten so bad, I was going to bed with two guns under my pillow. I knew I had to get out, or I was going to use those guns."

"Someone told me there was work in Sacramento, so I came up here. But that wasn't true. There was no work. Then I heard about the wasteland and here I am. I built this place from junk lumber to show people I still have skills and care and maybe it'll get me a job. But I never got another job, and now they're gonna evict us. Where am I supposed to go?"

Rainbow has a thyroid problem and suffers from obesity and rheumatoid arthritis and gets around using a walker. When the economy crashed, she got laid off and no one wanted to hire a fifty-something obese woman with medical problems. She now lives in "tent city."

Philip's wife has cancer, and they didn't have medical insurance. The bills kept piling up. They lost their home. They moved in with family and lived in their garage for a while. When Philip lost his job, they couldn't make the car payments anymore and overstayed their welcome with family. They had to move on. Now they live in "tent city."

Tina has learning disabilities since birth. Now forty-seven, she's outlived her mother who died of cancer and her father, who was an abusive alcoholic. She has no work skills. She was in a shelter but violated the rules by drinking, so she was evicted from the shelter. She now lives in "tent city."

Tiki worked in health care until she had a nervous breakdown. She never fully recovered. Her health benefits ran out. Then her unemployment checks ran out. Still suffering from depression and mental illness, no one will hire her. She has no money for rent. She lives in "tent city" now.

Coyote was a horse trainer his whole life. He got drunk one night and fought with one of his stablemates and that was it. He was fired. He lost his job. He has no severance pay. He can't pay rent. He now lives in "tent city."

John was a contractor. His father was a building inspector for Contra Costa county. Construction was booming in California. John was living "high off the hog." When the housing market first crashed in the late 80s, John was buried in debt and lost it all. He lost hope and checked out and made himself a little camp "on the island" in Discovery Park.

Boyd drove a truck for a day labor firm. Christina worked as a carney for a small, traveling amusement company, but her rheumatoid arthritis got too painful and she had to go on disability. They had a double-wide in Phoenix. Life was good.

Then Boyd got laid off and lost his income. Boyd's parents didn't like Christina and refused to help him financially as long he was with her. Boyd wouldn't dump his fiancé for his parents' money. They couldn't keep up payments on their double-wide. It was repossessed.

They packed everything into their van and drove west to Sacramento where Boyd grew up. But there was no work in Sacramento. They have lived in "tent city" for nine months now.

Carlos lost his job at Circuit City when the company declared bankruptcy in the crash. He lost his job and lost his unemployment benefits, and soon after that, he lost his apartment. He lives in "tent city" and he just got a job!

Karen is mentally challenged. I don't know her exact diagnosis, but she reminds me of a cousin of mine who is schizophrenic. She was discarded by her parents as a child. The shelters won't let her in with her cat. Her pet is all she has. She and her cat live in "tent city" now.

But the city is coming to close "tent city" and run everyone off the wasteland.

No one knows exactly when that will be. All they know is the shelters are full, and they have no place to go.

These are American citizens who need help.

Where are they supposed to live?

Just another fitful night of worrying.

Is today "the day"?

Are the police coming today?

Will we all be moved out today?

Will the mayor return my phone call today?

Will the governor return my phone call today?

Will God sweep down in Divine Intervention today?

Or is this just me being hopeful today?

~

I was so naïve when I moved into "tent city."

I believed that old saying that "the pen is mightier than the sword."

I believed that God had a purpose in mind when He called me to "give the homeless a voice."

I believed once the public saw fellow American citizens suffering in crisis and despair, they would rise up and help. Once they understood these people are veterans who have returned from war, unable to adapt to "normal" life, and the mentally ill who wander our streets trying to survive, help would come by the truckload.

But reality hit hard.

Based on the number of views on my videos – or lack of views, as it is in this case – it seems clear that no one wants to see homeless people online or in person.

The energy I'm observing is that the general public doesn't want homeless people on their streets anytime, anywhere, in any way, and doesn't want to hear about veterans, mental illness, disabilities, abuse, or neglect.

What I'm feeling here is hate and contempt, founded on ignorance, misunderstanding, and fear.

The feeling here on the streets is "Get those dirty bums out of here – now!"

Discovery John calls it NIMBY - "Not In My Back Yard!"

The public does not want to see mentally ill, disabled homeless people in their neighborhoods.

They would much rather see a bulldog skateboarding.

Everything's upside down.

Today in our own cities, towns, alleys, and doorsteps, we have over three and a half million homeless refugees - American citizens desperately in need of help.

Yet, instead of helping, we turn away.

I don't mean to be cynical, but have we *become so fearful and selfish that we no longer help our fellow man in need?*

Upside down!

Our parents and grandparents came from faraway lands with nothing in their pockets but a dream in their hearts. And our forefathers were homeless!

But today, we hate the homeless.

Upside down!

Why are there so many veterans out here on the streets? Is there really no public plan to provide mental health care for those who laid their life on the line for this country?

Really?

That's upside down!

I hear activists blame the government for slashing programs and that may be true. But in America we, the people, are the government. That means if we want change we must "be the change we wish to see."

But we don't change, we point fingers.

Everything's upside down.

I grew up *knowing* that Americans *always* help others in need. Whenever there is a crisis, anywhere around the world.

In the fourteen days I have been in "tent city," I count four church groups who have come to "tent city" with supplies, clothing, water, and food.

So, we point the finger of blame at the churches and the government.

But "we, the people," *are* the church *and* the government!

So, it all comes down to us, me and you.

Are we leading by example in our families and teaching our children to help others? Or are we so busy trying to make ends meet, that we relinquish the teaching of our children to teachers, schools, government, police, churches, TV, social media, and the computer?

Are we really too busy to guide the very lives we brought into this world?

Are we really too stressed to love one another?

It's all upside down!

~

It is late afternoon and gray clouds pile up as winds whip across the land. A crowd of "tent city" residents gathers under the dark threatening sky.

Boyd and Discovery John called an informal meeting of the Sacramento homeless population, from "tent city" to Discovery Island to the streets. John rode his bike to over 40 camps to encourage the "old" homeless to join the "new" homeless and discuss the possibility of taking a stand together for "Safe Ground."

"We called the meeting for this time because most people want to be back in their camps before dark," John informs me.

"It looks like maybe 30 or more people have shown up," I observe.

"That's a lot for homeless people. We tend to isolate and keep to ourselves. It's hard enough trying to hide yourself and dodge the cops. Groups of homeless people attract too much police attention."

With over 20 years homeless, he's got "street cred."

He takes the lead as organizer and spokesman for this gathering.

"Let's form a circle so we can all see and hear each other. This is our town hall meeting, without a town or a hall."

Everyone chuckles.

John's intelligence and leadership make me quickly forget I am listening to a pony-tailed, long-haired, scruffy-faced, bearded homeless dude. He sounds more like a savvy politician, and yet, he's homeless.

Why is this brilliant man homeless?

In the distance, I see two figures in long dark coats approaching the circle. The swirling winds lift the tails of their long coats, billowing and flapping with each step. As they get closer, I see it is an African-American couple.

I don't recognize them, but it's clear by their clothes, they are not homeless.

The man speaks first and introduces himself.

"Hello and peace. My name is Pastor Darrell. I pastor for the Church of Freedom and Hope, and we have come to offer our help."

Pastor Darrell's voice is strong and confident.

John speaks up, straight to the heart of the matter.

"We need water, sanitation, and a safe place to stay. The shelters are full. There is no place for us to go. We are tired of being moved around and harassed. We believe as taxpaying citizens we have a right to shelter. Can you help us with that?"

The homeless are naturally cynical and skeptical.

Pastor Darrell is calm and unruffled.

"That is why we came. This is my wife, Sharonda. Remember those port-a-johns that were delivered out here a few weeks ago? That was our church."

"But they took 'em away three days later!" someone shouts from the circle.

"That's right," says Pastor Darrell. "Right after we had those toilets delivered, we got a call from the city. They said if we didn't remove the toilets immediately, the church could be fined. We argued that every person needs a bathroom and that their threats were inhumane and uncivilized. We told the city it was our gift to the people at no cost to the city or the taxpayers but it fell on deaf ears. The city turned around and threatened to fine the rental company that delivered the toilets if they didn't remove them immediately. The rental company came out that day and removed the port-a-johns."

Voices from the circle spoke out.

"We heard the city said that the toilets were removed because the homeless people burned and trashed one of the toilets, which was not true at all!" one voice yelled.

"They said that by providing sanitation, it only encourages the homeless by making it easier on us," someone else called out.

Pastor Darrell listens and responds with his plan.

"We understand that. That is why we came to offer our help today. We are willing to take a stand with you. We will call in all our church members and other churches, from here to San Francisco to support this cause. We will bring microphones and speakers and music, and we will stay right here with you. We will even get arrested with you. We are prepared to do whatever it takes to get you the shelter, water, and sanitation you rightfully deserve, like every single citizen in this country."

Yells, claps, and cheers confirm agreement from the circle.

"We are willing to do that. We will take a stand with you against the inhumane treatment of all peoples. We will come here tomorrow and join forces with you, if that's what you all decide you want to do."

Pastor Darrell pauses for effect.

"Or we have another option. We have twelve acres of land and a building on the south side. It has electricity, running water, a kitchen, and bathrooms. We are prepared to house everyone there, right now."

Discovery John jumps in before the circle gets too enthusiastic with false hopes.

"Do you have a permit to house three hundred people? Otherwise, we will face the same eviction there that we are facing here. The city would never let that happen!"

Pastor Darrell remains cool under John's attack.

"No, we do not have a permit. But we do have a large, commercial kitchen. It is private land. And if we have to fight city hall for our personal right to house people, we are prepared to fight that fight."

"How far is it from Loaves and Fishes?"

"Does the light rail run nearby?"

"Is there public transportation?"

Most of the folks in the circle are wary and full of questions. It's a town meeting, and the citizens are passionately expressing their thoughts on freedom, liberty, and human rights.

Is this proactive citizens or homeless people?

As I listen to Pastor Darrell, it sounds like this could be a dream come true for "Safe Ground" – water, electricity, a big kitchen, twelve acres – a place for homeless people to be off the streets and begin rebuilding their lives again.

Pastor Darrell is persuasive, but the people decide they will take a vote after the pastor leaves and give him their answer tomorrow.

Pastor Darrell and his wife, Sharonda, thank everyone and shake hands, promising to return tomorrow for the decision from the people.

~

Discussions about Pastor Darrell go deep into the dusk. The consensus is that most people prefer to take a stand right here on the wasteland. Few are interested in Pastor Darrell's land with water and kitchen. It sounds nice on the surface, but many are skeptical of his proposal.

Besides, the land isn't close enough to the light rail, Loaves and Fishes, health care, SSI services, etc.

~

What do we do when a lawn mower is broken?

Do we keep pushing it across the lawn even though it doesn't cut anymore?

Or do we fix it?

Or get a new one?

What do we do when a system, an institution, a government is broken?

~

Pastor Darrell's plan reminds everyone of all the other promises they've heard.

"After Oprah was here, Governor Schwarzenegger came out to the wasteland and shook hands with us for all the local news cameras to see how compassionate and caring the Governor of California is. He promised help was on the way."

"Yeah, and the mayor came out, too, and shook hands and promised that help was on the way, too."

"Where are they now? They're nowhere to be found!"

"There ain't no help."

"They're all liars."

"They just send the cops. That's their help!"

"You think that Pastor's gonna be any different?"

They've seen it all. Smiling politicians saying whatever sounds good to the news cameras. False hopes and political double talk are what the homeless have heard for years. They've come to expect the lies, but that doesn't make it any easier.

Same shit, different day.

Will the pastor keep his word and take a stand on the wasteland with my homeless friends?

Will Pastor Darrell be any different from the phony politician talking heads?

Tuesday, April 14th

Boyd and Christina get up and leave camp at their usual oh-dark-thirty to go to work at Friendship Park.

I lay awake in my sleeping bag, feeling the darkness and the cold, worrying about what's going to happen here in Sacramento, what's going to happen to all these hurting people? And what I'm going to do?

Will Pastor Darrell and his wife show up with busloads of help from other churches as he promised and bring the public address system speakers and microphones to support the cause and stand strong for human rights?

Will the mayor and governor finally return my phone calls?

Or will the police come with trucks and bulldozers and push everyone off the wasteland?

~

Have you ever felt
Unwanted?
Ignored?
Misunderstood?
Disrespected?
Neglected?
Abused?
Deceived?
Discarded?
Now, imagine that you have no toilet, no running water, no place to sleep, and people looking at you with hate, everywhere you go.

How does it feel to be hated everywhere you go, constantly reminded that everyone hates you and wants you out of their sight?

That's what it feels like being homeless in America.

~

Three guys with clipboards from Lutheran Social Services show up at the wasteland around dusk, with news that there is going to be money to provide temporary group housing for about forty of the three hundred residents, if they sign up tonight. There will be "group homes" with 5–7 residents per home, as they begin the process of "social rehabilitation."

Boyd and Christina sign up right away. The wet winter, arthritis, and the stress of being homeless have taken its toll on the couple.

After nine months outside on the wasteland, Boyd is eager to get Christina inside. This may be the only chance they get to get out of the homeless rut and start to rebuild their lives.

Discovery John does not sign up for the housing plan.

~

If Boyd and Christina get housing, what will happen to the Safe Ground that Boyd began in "tent city"?

What will happen to me on the streets without Boyd as my guardian?

~

Car wheels crunching on the gravel of the levee rouse me from my racing thoughts and unanswered questions.

A black and white police car, followed by a black SUV roll up to our tents.

It's Batman and Robin, the "homeless" cops.

Discovery John speaks with them, since Boyd has already left for work.

Others gather around to hear the latest word from the cops.

"SMUD (*Sacramento Municipal Utility District*) will be coming with a survey crew today to stake out a fence line to fence off the high-power lines that you just moved out from under. They won't bother you up here. Just stay out of their way."

"What do they need to put up a fence for?" someone shouts out.

"It's for safety. It's not safe to be under those high-power lines," Officer Cooper aka Robin explains.

"We lived under those lines for the past year. No one was concerned for our safety then," shouts an angry voice.

"We understand. Now they are." Officer Cooper stays cool under fire.

"Will they leave us alone up here?" another voice asks.

"SMUD won't bother you up here. Just stay out of their way."

"Not SMUD. Will the city leave us alone?"

"We haven't gotten any orders, yet. That's all we know for now."

Little Mary stands five feet tall but her upset is ten feet tall, and she lets loose on Batman and Robin.

"The shelter beds are all full. You don't have anywhere to take us. Even if there were beds at the shelters, they won't allow me to bring my dog, and I'm not going anywhere without my dog! Where are we supposed to live?"

Batman and Robin have no answer.

"Take me to city hall. I'll camp across the street at Cesar Chavez until they have a place for me and my dog." Little Mary is adamant.

"Why don't they leave us alone? We're out of sight here on the wasteland," another angry voice chimes in.

"Take me to the capitol lawn. I'll stay at the capitol until they have a safe place for us to sleep." Mary crosses her arms, determined, taking a stand.

"You know we can't do that," Batman says. "We understand how tough this is for you. It's tough for us, too. All we can do is follow orders."

Batman and Robin come off as genuine, caring cops. Good people.

"We will have trucks and help you move all your belongings to make this as easy as possible on you."

Angry voices burst out in frustration.

"Take us where?"

"Where are we supposed to live?"

"I'm going back to the river. Screw this."

Batman and Robin do their best to listen and stay calm.

"Maybe you have family or friends who have an extra room or a garage who can help. Wherever you want to go, we'll get you there."

"Take me to the capitol!"

Discovery John finally speaks.

"What if we decide we don't want to move anymore, and we refuse to leave and stay right here?"

"Our orders say we have to clear the area."

"Why? You're the ones who told us to come here in the first place. Now, we have to move again? Where are we supposed to go?

"You're right. We did send you up here because it was out of sight. But now that it's all over the news and you're not out of sight anymore. We have new orders. We have to follow them, or we'll end up without a job. We wish there was something we could do."

"What if we just stay right here?"

"We don't want to have to arrest anyone. We'd rather do this peacefully with everyone's cooperation."

Redwood is fuming mad.

"I'm not going anywhere! I'll chain myself to the fence. I just got out of jail. This is the only place I have. I'm not going anywhere until I have a place to sleep."

"We understand. We don't make the rules. We just enforce them."

Batman and Robin – Zoulas and Cooper – are trained professionals. They remain cool under fire. They know most of these people. They see them every day down at Loaves and Fishes.

"This sucks! Where are we supposed to go?"

"Screw this. I'm a taxpayer. I'm gonna go camp on the capitol lawn until they come up with a safe place for me to be."

"We'll do our best to help you to make this as painless as possible."

"When? When?"

"Right now, they have not told us the date but the plans are in place to bring trucks and bulldozers and move you all out, most likely sometime this week, in the next few days."

"Move us where? We have no place to go!"

"We wish we could help with that. We're just following orders."

"That's what they said at Auschwitz! They were just following orders, too."

"We just came by to give you a heads up. Do what you've got to do. We'll be here to help you move when the time comes."

Batman and Robin leave in their SUV.

Agitated like a hive of angry bees, they buzz and spit and curse their way across the tracks to Loaves and Fishes.

At least Sister Libby will welcome them with open arms and a smile... and coffee, sweet rolls, and a safe place for the day.

~

What am I going to do with my tent and sleeping bag and clothes when the city comes to move everyone out of "tent city" in a few days?

I'm beginning to sound like I'm homeless.

~

Boyd is at the Day Storage Shed, just like every other day, greeting each person with a "Hey, brother" or "Hey, sister" and a hug.

Christina is on the food line, serving each guest with a smile, "What would you like? A muffin, a roll, or cake? Or one of each?"

I grab a coffee and a bran muffin and head over to my office.

Time to upload my footage and edit my daily report.

~

A veteran who chose to remain anonymous told me that when he was in the service, the sergeant told them "when to wake, when to shit, when to march."

"I don't know how to do things without being ordered. I can go to war and kill because I was trained to do that. I hardly know what to do without orders. No one trained me to take care of a house or be a husband."

Wow!

Trained to kill but not trained to live.

Maybe we should be training our soldiers to live after the killing is done.

Just a thought.

~

I joke to Boyd that I have a production studio in the trunk of my car.

I don't even want to imagine what I would do if I were homeless without a car.

164

~

My "Live from Tent City" post today will call for immediate action.

If someone with heart has a piece of land where these 300 disabled, unwanted refugee citizens could go, a catastrophe could be turned into a miracle.

We need a miracle at this point.

Pastor Darrell offered land and a commercial kitchen yesterday. Will he show up today?

~

The city fathers are determined to send the police to move us out of "tent city" by the end of the week.

What will that mean to me and my film efforts?

Where will I live?

I don't have money for a contingency plan B to hold up in a motel.

Will Boyd be there to protect me, or will I be on the streets on my own?

Whatever the case, I don't have time to worry or plan, so I do my best to stay focused on my filming and editing.

I'm a willing and humble servant, God, but after two weeks here, I'm not sure how long I can last.

I guess I have to trust that God has something planned for me.

I just I wish I knew what that was.

~

Back in my office, the coffee is tepid and the muffin stale. The batteries are charging and the computer and hard drive are connected to the camera. I log the footage of Pastor Darrell. He's very persuasive in his appeal to take a stand and fight for homeless rights.

I thought his offer of land and building was great, but most of the residents, including Boyd and John, are skeptical and suspicious.

Will Pastor Darrell do what he promised?

I sure hope so.

Boyd comes in.

"Hey, brother, I told you to keep the door locked."

"I know, brother. My bad."

"I just got word that SMUD is already up there with machines."

I look at my watch. It's 8:07.

"Wow. They didn't waste any time. Did you hear what they're doing? Do you think I should go up and film?"

"I don't know, brother. That's your call. I just heard, and I wanted to tell you right away, in case you wanted to go up and film it."

"Thanks, brother. You da man."

"No, you da man. I'm just a messenger. Are you gonna go film 'em?"

"I don't know. I guess. I gotta figure it out. I can't be editing and filming at the same time. Probably."

"I just wanted to let you know. I gotta get back to work."

"Thanks, brother."

"And lock the door, please," Boyd says in a chuckle locking the door on his way out.

Thank God, Boyd has my back.

I sit down and stare at my work.

What should I do?

I stop.

I pray for God to guide my steps.

~

The machines are coming to eliminate the humans.

I feel like a soldier going off to battle.

I've got twenty, maybe thirty pounds of gear on my shoulder.

My weapon is my camera.

The battle is from the heart, helping others fight the advancing machines.

How many dollars and man hours will be spent evicting the homeless?

What if those dollars could be spent to help and heal?

Will the mayor call?

Will the governor intervene?

Will Pastor Darrell and choirs of angels appear?

Will a secret benefactor show up in the nick of time with land and money to save the day and give shelter and dignity to these refugees?

Or will there be more machines and more police?

~

I heard they are erecting barbed-wire cyclone fences around the wasteland so no humans can breech this toxic dump ever again.

It's all upside down.

~

Boyd gave me good information. He must have good sources.

As I crest the rise over the tracks, I see three white SMUD trucks, trailers, backhoe, and bobcat working near the spot we had vacated two days before.

A survey crew is laying out the fence line, while the bobcat drills post holes with a giant drill bit, followed by a man who places a steel fence post in each hole. There is already a line of a dozen posts, slanting in the holes, ready for the impending concrete to stand them up straight.

Off to the left stands a newly erected 2-foot by 6-foot steel sign on two 8' high steel posts.

"PRIVATE PROPERTY"
"VIOLATORS WILL BE PROSECUTED"
"KEEP OUT"

Clearly the city is set on implementing the plan that Batman and Robin described earlier this morning. Sweep the wasteland of all people and tents and erect fences to put an end to this pubic image fiasco called "tent city," and stop the international media clamoring for pictures of the current economic collapse in the capital of California.

In our modern age, we're all about image and branding. Homeless people are not the face Sacramento wants to show the whole world. It's bad press for Sacramento in particular, and California in general. This PR blight needs to be gone – *now*!

~

I talk to a couple of the SMUD workers and tell them I am filming a documentary about "tent city." They don't want to be interviewed on camera, so I put the cover on the lens.

I ask them what the purpose of the fence is. They tell me "off the record" they were sent to erect a fence to protect the public from future accidents or harm because it is unsafe to be under the high-power lines.

But it was okay for homeless people to sleep under them before this?

I film close-ups of the six-foot long drill boring holes in the earth and wide shots of the empty wasteland and the new fence. There must be fifty posts in the ground by the time I finish filming, and I head back to Friendship Park to continue editing today's piece.

They're moving very quickly.

I don't think I'll be hearing from the mayor or the governor.

No sign of Pastor Darrell or all his churches, either.

Looks like it might be time to get to work on Plan B.
Where are all these people going to go?
And what about me?
Where am I going to go?

~

As I return to Friendship Park, it is clear that everybody on the street already knows that SMUD is erecting fences on the wasteland.

It feels like a fight could break out any second.

The park is pulsing with panic and stress.

People see me with my camera on my shoulder, and they want to know what I've seen. I don't want to be incendiary, so I try to choose my words wisely.

"It's just like Batman and Robin said this morning. The survey crew and fence crew are erecting a fence around the high-power lines."

"Are they messing with anybody's stuff?" an angry voice asks.

"Nope, they haven't touched anybody's stuff that I saw. Just digging holes and putting in posts for the fence."

Fortunately, Boyd saves me from further questions with a friendly arm around my shoulder. Nobody's gonna mess with me when Boyd's around. He escorts me to my office, my camera and tripod on one shoulder, his strong arm on my other.

"I love you, little brother."

"Love you, too, brother."

"And lock the door. Please."

Boyd chuckles with his hearty ha, ha, ha.

A big man with a big laugh - and a big heart.

"Yes, sir."

"And stop calling me sir!"

"Yes, sir."

Laughter is our only defense against the harsh reality of the eviction facing us.

Where are we going to go?

~

Emotion, uncertainty, and stress are trying to take over my mind, but I have to get this day's post edited and posted. There is a one-in-a-million chance a benevolent philanthropist will see it and respond immediately with power, influence, money, and land to save these folks from chaos and more suffering.

Why is Sacramento – a government of, by, and for the people – spending hundreds of thousands of tax dollars evicting homeless people and erecting fences?

Don't they realize that housing and treating the mentally ill would cost far less?

The only thing keeping me from losing it and going postal is my commitment to give these people a voice. If it were up to me, I'd admit my failure, pack up my gear, and head home.

But since I made a promise to God, I have to keep my word and do my best, so I immerse myself in my work and ignore the frantic voices inside my head telling me to get the heck out of Dodge.

Something is very wrong here!

My camera and I may not be big enough to fix it.

Everything's upside down.

~

I lost over an hour of editing time going up to the wasteland to film the SMUD crew.

So, I skip the lunch break again.

Boyd brings me a salad and some fruit from the Loaves cafeteria.

What a guy!

Inside this bear of a beast is a heart of gold, filled with love.

~

Focused, in the zone, not even stopping for a bathroom break, I rush to finish the edit before 3 o'clock when the park closes.

Maybe this story will be the key that unlocks human compassion and stops the freight train of ignorance and hate from its final destination of Eviction Station.

Or maybe, it will be one more ignored youtube video, just like the other thirteen stories I've posted so far.

I may not have captured the public's eye as of yet, but I have noticed a large swell of confidence and unity among my homeless friends. They are rallying behind Boyd and John's leadership. They are tired of being harassed and herded like animals. They are going to take a stand to fight for their rights. They are human beings and deserve to be treated just like every other American citizen.

That may all change when the bulldozers show up.

~

I don't know how I will continue this work without a place to stay in "tent city."

I don't have money for a motel.

Where will I go?

I guess I'm gonna have to believe God will provide.

~

With all the stress and nerves throughout the park, I decide to film while I have daylight and post the "Live from Tent City" report to youtube later, after it gets dark.

Boyd helps me carry my computer and hard drive back to my car for safe storage while I carry the camera, tripod, and backpacks.

"You think Pastor Darrell will show?" I ask hopefully.

"Forget about him. He'll never show." Boyd replies matter-of-factly.

"Why do you say that?"

"After nine months on the wasteland, I think I've seen most everything. There have been other preachers who came and promised help and never showed. Schwarzenegger came out after Oprah and shook hands and promised help. The mayor came and promised help, too. Where are they now? And what do we got for all their promises? Nothin'."

There is nothing I can say.

"Pastor Darrell isn't comin', either. I'll bet you money on that."

I totally understand Boyd's feelings.

Broken promises hurt.

When I grew up, I was taught I always had to keep my word. If I made a promise to someone, I had to keep my promise, or I was not a man of my word and not to be trusted.

It used to be a mark of character to be a "man of your word."

Today, it's different.

Character has been replaced by personal agendas and greed.

Politicians and world leaders "spin" a story to make themselves look good, then change their mind if the situation suits. The new ethic of today's world leaders is to do or say whatever it takes to get the desired results, at any cost.

Presidents lie.

Senators cheat.

Congressmen steal.

Governors deceive.

Businessmen scam.

The "new" Golden Rule states: "He who has the most money rules."

What's honesty got to do with it?

If I don't get caught – I win!

Really?

These are the politicians we elected, the leaders we follow, the businesses we support, and the churches we attend?

What does our acceptance of their unethical behavior say about us and our society, our community, and our families?

What have we become?

~

The SMUD crews are gone when I return to "tent city."

Two lines of steel stakes are in the ground for the new safety fence. The huge, steel NO TRESPASSING sign stands over the empty wasteland.

The machines are gone for the night, but they'll be back tomorrow.

~

A dozen or so are gathered around Discovery John laying out the guidelines for taking a stand.

"If you are on parole or wearing an ankle bracelet, you probably don't want to stand and fight because there's a good chance you will be arrested, which means that you've violated your parole and you're going back to jail. Don't be stupid. Live to fight another day. Let me see a show of hands of who's going to take a stand here on the wasteland and fight – and are ready to get arrested."

About half dozen hands go up.

Six people are ready to take a stand for human rights and the right to a safe place to sleep.

No sign of Pastor Darrell. Or the governor or mayor, for that matter. So much for promises.

~

I struggle trying to get my mind to think straight.

I film until the sun sets, then head off to the library to upload my post for the day. I park outside the Sacramento Public Library at Ninth and I Streets. The library is closed, but I sit in the car and use their wifi to upload today's post of "Live from Tent City: Day 14".

How ironic that as my laptop does its thing uploading my HD video file to youtube, outside my car window are the people of the streets, the very people for whom I came here to give a voice.

I feel impotent and overcome with a feeling of failure. Tears of despair stream down my cheeks.

What the hell am I supposed to do now?

I pray.

"God, these people need a miracle. I've done what you've asked me to do. I've given your people a voice. But few people watch my videos. No one seems to care about the homeless except Sister Libby. Tell me what to do. I'm lost. Make my heart strong and guide my steps so that I can serve You and serve these people who need so much help. Thank you, God, for keeping me strong. Amen."

What will tomorrow bring?

Wednesday, April 15th

What do we do with the poor and needy?

What do we do with the mentally ill?

What do we do with disabled veterans?

We call them homeless and we hate them.

We hate them because they are dirty and disgusting.

We hate them because they scare us.

We hate them because we could end up like them.

We're only a paycheck away from being broke ourselves.

And we know what happens when we can't pay our bills...

I am here in "tent city" with my camera and tripod, waiting for the final eviction, wondering what the hell happened to the world I grew up in.

We were taught to help our neighbors.

What happened?

When did we stop helping each other?

When did we decide to arrest the mentally ill?

Arrests do not solve the problem nor do they address the source of the "homeless" issue. We pay millions of dollars every year in taxes to jail homeless people without solving or improving the problem.

In business, wasting money demands new strategies to cut losses and improve profitability.

In government, politicians are no longer accountable to the people who elected them, so they waste money recklessly.

Bottom line, if we took care of our mentally ill and veterans and housed them instead of dumping them on the streets, we would save money and radically reduce the homeless problem in America.

So why don't we do it.

The world is upside down.

~

The Hopi Indians have only two laws, "Try to understand things, and don't go around hurting each other."

The Dalai Lama said, "Our main purpose in life is to help one another. If we cannot help one another, let us not hurt one another."

Jesus taught, "Love your neighbor as yourself."

What do we do?

We fear the homeless and call the police!

Really?

Upside down.

Jesus would be arrested today for aiding and abetting the homeless and feeding the poor without a license from the health department.

Fear is life without love.

Who would want to live that way?

Upside down.

~

The police are here.

Black and whites, sheriffs, park rangers, bulldozers, dump trucks, garbage trucks, and three white "Corrections" buses full of inmates in orange jumpsuits.

They assemble on the site of the old "tent city" that we vacated four days before.

The SMUD crew is already here, drilling and setting fence posts for the new cyclone fence.

Government officials are present this morning to supervise the clean-up of the public image mess, but no mayor or governor. The low, threatening rumble of the dozers and dump trucks means the eviction has begun and "tent city" will soon be gone.

If this were Rwanda or Zimbabwe, the U.S. would be here with medical supplies, doctors, tents, toilets, social workers, water, and food to help the refugees in crisis.

But our own American refugees here at home are labeled "dirty, drunken bums," and we send the police to get them out of our sight.

Why don't we help them?

It's all *upside down.*

~

As expected, Batman and Robin are the front men for the eviction operation, approaching the last two tents standing in the old "tent city" to see if there are people still inside, while hungry bulldozers idle nearby.

Two squads of orange-suited inmates with rubber gloves and garbage bags fan out under the supervision of armed guards to hand pick what the dozers can't get.

As I'm filming and recording, I wonder what has become of the America I love. I am downright disgusted.

How we treat our fellow citizens in this time of crisis makes me sick to my stomach.

If this is what Americans do to Americans, do I really want to be an American anymore?

~

Crossing the tracks in the distance is a small group of people in green jackets and caps.

It's Sister Libby and the green hats from Friendship Park! They have come to support the residents who are being evicted. Sister Libby wears her usual loving smile.

She is not afraid of the bulldozers or the police. She leads her band of volunteers through the sea of inmates and cops. The homeless residents watch with guarded hope as Sister Libby and her band of green hats approach.

People rush and surround Sister Libby to thank her for coming. Sister Libby shares hugs with each person, one by one, taking the time to look them in the eye and tell them God loves them.

Libby addresses the group.

"Let's all join hands and form a circle and pray. Lord knows we need all the help we can get today."

Her touch of love and dash of humor transforms the morning gloom and doom into hope.

"Father God, you say in your word that wherever two or more are gathered together, you are there. We are gathered here today in this circle to thank You for being here with us, and for making us strong with Your love and courage."

"We need a Safe Ground here in Sacramento, Lord. All the shelter beds are full. There are more people losing their homes every day. These people have no place to go. We need a Safe Ground, Lord."

"We have come here today to take a stand and support our friends without homes. We will stand here together with you, and we will not leave Sacramento until there is a Safe Ground for all people to be safe. Amen."

Three hundred yards west down the levee is their counterpart, a circle of police, sheriffs, rangers, and corrections officers planning their next move.

Prayers or police, which one will win?

As the prayer circle disperses, Sister Libby and John head down the levee to discuss the issues at hand with the commanding officers.

The bulldozers and inmates continue their sweep across the wasteland. There's nothing to do but wait and see what the cops say to Sister Libby and John.

Glenn, one of the volunteers pulls a guitar from a weathered black case, puts the strap over his shoulder, and tunes it up.

"I wrote this song about your struggle here in "tent city." It's called "America, America.""

Glenn strums his guitar and sings,

"America, America to me it makes no sense.

Your houses are all empty and your people live in tents.

America, America, how did things get this way?

Got out of touch and gave it up

Then you gave it all away."

~

I flash on John Steinbeck's "Grapes of Wrath."

America has been here before, in the Great Depression when millions were without jobs, homes, or shelter. Those times were filled with fear and loathing for the jobless masses, too.

We sent the police then and we send the police now.

Did someone say something about "history repeating itself"?

~

Fear breeds hate.

Fear says, "These poor people might come knocking on my door. What will I do? I can't feed them all, I'd better call the police now!"

Love says, "These people are hurting and need help. I have a little food in the freezer. It's not much, but it might help."

Love brings people together.

~

Who would ever want to end up with no place to sleep, no place to wash, no place to go to the bathroom?

That would really suck!

I've only been here sixteen days, but I can tell you without a doubt that you DO NOT want to be homeless – EVER!

You don't ever want to end up on the street.

You don't ever want to be disabled or mentally ill or a veteran with PTSD, returning from war, unable to adjust on the mean streets of reality.

The streets are filled with anger and hate today.

They are not a nice place to be for you, your family, or your friends.

~

This is a crisis.

We got here because we didn't know how to deal with our mentally ill.

~

Sister Libby and John bring news from the police back to the waiting circle.

John speaks first.

"We spoke with the captain and asked her directly if the police have orders to arrest those who refuse to leave. The captain explained that we are trespassing on private land and trespassing is against the law. She would not come right out and say they will arrest those who refuse to leave, but she said we were violating the law."

Sister Libby chimes in with clarification.

"For now, the captain said the police are here to supervise the vacating of the land according to the law. It does not appear anyone will be arrested today. So, for one more night, we are all still free."

As the sun goes down, the dozers go quiet. The garbage trucks leave. The orange-suited inmates are herded back on to the white buses by the cops in blue, returning to the gray prison for the black night.

As the police get into their patrol cars, three cars head west into the sinking sun, while two squad cars do a final drive-by past the circle of people at the radio tower.

Sister Libby shares hugs with all the residents and promises to come back with more help in the morning.

There's a peculiar mixed bag of energy in the air. There is a quiet resignation, a knowing that "tent city" is over. The comfort of shared community is shattered. It may not be gone yet, but it is going, that is certain.

It will soon be every man for himself, survival alone on the mean streets.

And every woman for herself, too!

~

Some people wander back to their tents, while others settle into their chairs in the circle and gaze out into the coming darkness. No one talks. There's nothing to say. Everyone knows, this is the end.

As people withdraw into the reality of their solitary uncertainties, the land is blanketed in indigo twilight ringed with fear.

The hope is gone.

They don't need to talk anymore.

There is only time to worry and focus on the unknown.

What will they do with all the stuff they can't carry?

What's going to happen to their pets?

Where will they go now?

Thursday, April 16th

I didn't sleep very well.

It was a night of uncertainty.

Yesterday was the first day in two weeks I did not file a report of Live from Tent City.

Do I stay with the folks while the bulldozers and police are here, or do I leave to edit and post another report of Live from Tent City?

I made an executive decision.

I chose to stand in solidarity with my down and out homeless friends and stay to film whatever happened.

I will edit and post yesterday's report today or tomorrow.

It's not as if the free world is waiting and wondering what's happening with all these homeless refugees in Sacramento. Nobody's watching anyway.

We've got enough damn problems in this world without having to worry about worthless homeless bums!

I'm sorry to be so negative and cynical.

I'm frustrated, confused, and angry as hell!

Where did all the love go?

~

Fear says, "We don't have enough."
Love says, "There's plenty for all. Help that person."
It's one or the other.
Which do you choose?
Fear?
Or love?
It's your choice.

~

What do presidents, soldiers, and homeless people all have in common?

They cope with stress 24/7/365.

There are no days off when you're at war.

There are no days off when you're the President.

There are no days off when you're homeless.

You must be sharp and alert, totally aware, always on edge, ready for the next surprise, not knowing where it will come from or when it will go down.

You can't ever let your guard down.

Sleep with one eye open.

Ready at all times.

The only difference between presidents, soldiers, and homeless people is that presidents and soldiers have shelter, food, water, sanitation, and support.

Homeless people have nothing.

~

As dawn breaks on this fifteenth day of my mission, it is clear help is not forthcoming.

The governor isn't coming.

The mayor isn't coming.

Pastor Darrell and choirs of angels are not coming.

This is the end of "tent city" in Sacramento.

But it is not the end of homelessness.

Tent cities will pop up all across America, as more people lose their jobs and homes.

My heart is aching with grief.

I feel so helpless.

I've given the homeless a voice, and the world couldn't care less.

It is indifferent.

I feel like I want to break down and cry.

But there is no time for tears or self-pity right now.

It's time to be prepared for the worst.

Who knows what's going to happen next?

The police are back.

The white buses and orange-suited inmates are back.

The bulldozers and sanitation trucks are back rumbling and rolling.

The media is here, transmission towers raised as reporters and cameramen prepare to report the leading news story of the day.

This "tent city" is dead.

~

When I moved in several weeks ago, there were hundreds of tents with two hundred and fifty to three hundred people.

After weeks of fear and threats, it's now down to about thirty-five to forty tents, with maybe seventy people still remaining this morning.

Of the seventy homeless residents remaining, most are in some phase of tearing down or packing up, resigned to the reality that they can't stay here anymore.

New fences are going up to keep homeless out.

People are fleeing with what they can carry, leaving behind whatever they can't fit on their bikes, wagons, carts, backs, or in trash bags.

Bulldozers claw and level what has been left behind.

They must leave this place, and they must leave now.

Where will they go?

Who knows?

Who cares?

It's upside down.

Where are the leaders in this crisis of unnecessary human suffering?

How could any mayor, governor, or president ignore the fact that 27% of the homeless population are veterans? How can we not at least help our veterans?

"But ask yourself, what American president, politician, celebrity, athlete, or leader has taken a stand to address homelessness in our civilized nation?"

I couldn't come up with one name.

Not one.

Could it really be true that not one leader in this great country has taken a stand against the abomination of homelessness?

We need to help these people.

The time for compassion and change is now.

We cannot afford to look away any longer.

~

Most of the "tent city" residents are already resigned to a losing outcome. They are packing all their gear and getting ready to move on. Even those who decide to make a stand for human rights, or risk getting arrested, will not be staying here.

It's time to move on.

Boyd created a community of people helping people in "tent city." Those down on their luck helped others down on theirs.

Now, they've all given up. Reluctance, anguish, frustration, and anger are in their every step and action.

~

The only way to make the homeless disappear is to help them.

Many do not have the tools, skills, or resources to help themselves.

As long as we continue to herd, harass, and arrest, NOTHING WILL CHANGE!

After all the man-hours in jail and court are expended and paid for, what has been accomplished? The homeless are back on the streets with no place to go. With the waste of human resources and so many taxpayer dollars, it is no wonder our cities and states are bankrupt.

The definition of insanity is "doing the same thing over and over and expecting different results."

From where I stand, our government is insane!

Will there ever be a leader who will take a stand to reform how we treat our mentally ill, disabled, and homeless in America?

Continuing the policies that haven't worked for 50 years will not solve the problem.

And yet, here are the bulldozers and police, right here, right now.

It's all *upside down and it may never get right side up again.*

~

A reporter from the Associated Press asks Boyd for an interview.

Boyd is breaking down their site and packing their gear.

"Sure, you can talk to me, but I'm gonna keep on working. The bulldozers are comin' and we've got to move."

"That's fine. How did you end up homeless? What happened?" Asks Mr. AP.

"I've worked my whole life. I've paid taxes my whole life. I was driving a truck for a day labor company in Phoenix. When the economy collapsed, I lost my job. I was estranged from my parents. They gave me a choice. If I left my fiancé, they would help me financially. I wasn't about to leave Christina. Since I grew up in Sacramento, we came here. But there was no work here, either. That's how we ended up homeless with no place to sleep."

"How long have you been here?"

"Honey, is it eight months or nine months that we're here? I forget. It's been a long, cold winter, that's for sure."

"Why didn't you stay at a shelter?"

"Shelters don't let unmarried couples stay together. I wasn't gonna let us be separated. That's the worst thing that could happen. She's got diabetes. So, we set up here in "tent city." It was cool with the cops. In fact, they were the ones who told us about the wasteland."

"What's the wasteland?"

"That's where we're standing right now. It used to be a dump for the Blue Diamond Almond factory. But since Oprah came, now the media calls it "tent city." I guess they thought that was a catchier name than the wasteland."

Boyd chuckles to himself.

"So, where are you headed now that they're evicting you from the wasteland?"

"We don't know where we're gonna go. I've worked my whole life and paid my taxes every year. I'm a veteran. I served my country. And this is what we get for service to our country? It used to be it didn't matter whether you were a Christian or a Buddhist or a Muslim, we were all Americans, and we helped our neighbors and gave to the needy, and the poor. I still work. I work part-time at Loaves and Fishes, and Christina volunteers serving breakfast. And now the police are here to move us out because the politicians say we have to go."

"Are you mad?"

"I'm not mad. I'm upset. I forgive the politicians. I forgive the police. It's not the police's fault. They're just following orders. They're just doing their jobs. But the politicians, they say one thing and do another. That used to be called a lie. The mayor was out here. The governor, too. They both promised to help. But they never helped. Where are they now?"

"This used to be a God-fearing nation. Not anymore. Today, we fear strangers, terrorists, and the homeless. Does anyone know what homeless even means? Most of these people out here are disabled or mentally ill. We've got a lot of veterans out here who laid their lives on the line for this country and now this is how we treat them?"

"You know, Jesus didn't come to serve the politicians and the rich. Jesus served the poor, the downtrodden, the outcasts, the sick. Jesus served people like us."

"All of us will have to go before our Creator and answer for our actions. I forgive the politicians and the police, but what they're doing here still isn't right."

"It looks like you're packing up to move. Do you know where are you moving to?"

"Nope. All we know is we can't stay here because the police have told us to move or we'll be arrested."

In the face of police and bulldozers, hope for an immediate solution is fading fast.

Most everybody is fretful, tearing down their tents and packing their belongings in the realization that this ship is going down.

Discovery John packs his gear into plastic shopping bags that he can secure to his bike with bungee cords.

Tom and Annie sort through piles of belongings they load into a shopping cart, while their tired old dog, Trouble, looks on with sad eyes.

Little Mary stacks her gear neatly in piles as her lab puppy pants and paws with playful puppy energy.

James lashes heavily-loaded rolling carts and wagons together with rope to form a baggage train of his life belongings.

Kennedy, a Harley do-rag on his head, his arms and neck tattooed, squats on his gear beside his bike puffing on his cigarette.

A lone American flag behind him flaps easily in the light breeze.

This former dump, this wasteland, this "tent city" was once a community, a place of safety, a place of security without fights or violence, where people helped one another.

They made the best of a bad situation and called it home.

Not anymore.

"Give me your tired, your poor… the homeless… I lift my lamp beside the Golden door."

The Golden door of the Golden State is now closed to the tired, the homeless and the poor.

~

Sister Libby calls everyone together on the levee for a prayer circle of those remaining, mostly those who are prepared to be arrested if it should come to that.

"Oh, Lord, we are gathered here today to thank you for the love and community we have shared. As we face new struggles, challenges, and hurdles, we ask you to guide our steps in Jesus name. Amen."

"I've been talking with the police captain, and they have made it clear that they do not want to arrest anyone, but today is the last day. If anyone doesn't leave the wasteland by tonight, they will have no option but to arrest those in violation."

There are a lot of stunned and confused faces in the prayer circle.

"I know that we talked about making a stand here, but the police are asking everyone to pack up and leave peacefully. We are hidden away from the public here and no one cares. So next Monday, we will take our "Safe Ground" plan to the state capitol and the governor for all the world to see. We will not leave Sacramento until there is "Safe Ground" for everyone to sleep."

Shocked by the surprise turn of events, there is strained silence in the prayer circle, until Redwood can't hold it in anymore.

"This is bullshit! You say you're gonna come out here and take a stand with us and ain't gonna leave until we have "Safe Ground" for everyone to sleep and now you're telling us to leave. This is bullshit! We're supposed to just pack up and leave because we don't want to upset the police. Screw that! I'm staying. Fuck that! Let them arrest me and send me back to jail."

Boyd lumbers over to his friend, Redwood, and puts an arm around his shoulder.

"I know you're pissed. I understand. Believe me, I feel the same way. But what good is it going to do getting arrested? And you go back to county for breaking parole? You're screwed."

"I'm screwed any way you look at it. What difference does it make if they send me back now or send me back later? Here I am, trying to be a good citizen and get my life together, and now the police want to arrest me for sleeping. Fuck that!"

"Look, little brother, I know how you feel. But if you stay and get arrested, that means I have to stay and get arrested with you and then what do I do about Christina? I can't help her or you or me in jail. What else are we gonna do? Getting arrested doesn't make sense."

"Fuckin' nothin' makes sense right now!"

"I know, little brother, I know."

With his big arm around Redwood's shoulder, Boyd gently steers Redwood off the levee away from the rest of the people.

Worried silence settles over the people under the drone of bulldozers.

It's over.

There will be no fight.

There will be no stand for a safe place to sleep.

People finish packing their gear. Some load their bikes and carts and head out. Others just squat and wait for the police to take them away to who knows where.

Enut confides in me.

"It's just another broken promise. People say they're gonna stand with us even if they have to be arrested, but when push comes to shove, they're runnin' instead of standin'. What's this world comin' to when you can't even count on nuns anymore? At least they feed us and give us a place to rest during the day. You can't trust anyone anymore."

~

Throughout the day, police, trucks, and flatbeds roll into camp and load up with a few more peoples' gear and truck it away.

Sister Libby has provided temporary storage in a shipping container at Loaves and Fishes, so most of the personal property being removed from the wasteland goes to Loaves until people can sort out where they are going from here.

Inmates in orange jumpsuits sweep through the camps making piles for the dozers to eat. Dozers scoop, scrape, and dump the remains into garbage trucks to be hauled off to the dump, a different one than the one these people have been living on.

By late afternoon, there are only six tents left standing.

Boyd is loading their gear into his car.

"We're going to stay at the Motel 6 tonight. You should get a room, too."

I haven't really thought about what I am going to do once this all unravels here in Sacramento, but I know for my wellbeing and safety, I need to stay close to Boyd.

Right now, I wouldn't know what to do without my guardian.

I quickly do a mental check of my budget; I have enough left for a $42.00 room at the Motel 6 for one night. After that, I'll be staying in my car.

I have come to give the homeless a voice, and now, I'm facing homelessness myself.

What am I supposed to do now, God?

~

I load my camping equipment and camera gear into my car and follow Boyd and Christina down the levee.

The whole scene is surreal.

The wasteland is empty, stripped clean by the dozers and crews.

Where we used to sit on the logs and talk with Reno and Ronn at the end of a day, there's a new line of posts, set in concrete and ready for the cyclone fencing to go up to keep people out for evermore.

The city is determined to remove any and all remnants of the "tent city" Oprah made internationally famous.

Bravo, Sacramento, you have just spent hundreds of thousands of taxpayer dollars and cleared a toxic dump of homeless people.

And there's a new fence, too!

~

Where do 300 homeless people go when there are no shelter beds and no place for them to sleep?

Tomorrow, when you go to work and there's a homeless man sleeping in your doorway, you'll know where he came from.

~

Boyd and Christina and I rent the last two rooms available at the Motel 6.

Like teenagers on spring break, we order a pizza and "party" in our motel room. Boyd, Christina, and me in the Motel 6, eating pizza and drinking beer.

Par-tay!

Woo-hoo!

It's more like a wake than a party. We are grateful to be alive and under roof, but concerned and worried about all those who are still outside.

It's a jungle out there.

Alone on the street with no friends to watch your back.

No security, no safety, no place to call home.

Constant anxiety, uncertainty, and fear.

This is what it is to be homeless in America today.

I pray it never happens to you, your family, or your friends.

And I pray especially for all who suffer from mental illness, especially our veterans who return from war, unable to cope and end up on the streets.

~

How nice it is to take a hot shower and walk around naked with central heat.

Then the guilt sweeps in and annihilates all the warm fuzzy feelings.

~

There are people out there who don't have a hot shower tonight.

I came to give them a voice and no one heard.

They are still on the street.

Now, what am I going to do?

EPILOGUE

I ended up staying in Sacramento for 38 months. I could not desert my friends in need.

I filmed marches, committee meetings, protests, interviews, breakfasts, "Safe Ground" camps, city council meetings, rallies, fundraisers, promotions, screenings, dinners, lunches, seminars, symposiums, births, deaths, breakdowns, breakthroughs, failures, and successes.

I ran out of money, closed my apartment in Thousand Oaks, put everything in storage, declared bankruptcy, and became homeless myself.

From what I've seen, there are hundreds of thousands of mentally ill men and women on our streets, because we have failed to house and care for them. None of us like seeing them begging on street corners and camped under bridges. It is hurting our communities, our families, and our hearts.

A little bit of kindness and understanding goes a long way to begin the healing of our mentally ill and substantially reducing our "homeless" population at the same time.

An L.A. County Deputy Sheriff told me that 30% of the population at the L.A. County Jail are mentally ill.

Why are we incarcerating our mentally ill?

~

I moved into "tent city" with my camera in 2009. Very little has changed in those nine years; in fact, the situation has gotten worse.

If our government isn't going to change, then we the people, who elect the government, must make the change.

We must get all the veterans and mentally ill off the streets and into housing immediately. The "Safe Ground" model, using tiny homes would be a quick and cost-effective solution. Tiny houses are being used in Utah, Washington and other states, but not yet California.

Some estimates say the homeless population could be reduced by as much as 65% or more by housing and helping our veterans and our mentally ill.

~

June 1, 2012, I left Sacramento, emotionally, psychologically, and spiritually drained. I could no longer stay, lest depression and sadness consume my spirit and heart.

I went to Death Valley to talk to God.

I stood naked at the gates of hell.

There was more work to do.

Here is that work - these "tent city" diaries.

If my story opened your eyes and touched your heart, take action!

Pass it on, tell a friend. Write your congressman, senator, and the President.

Tell them we need to take care of our veterans and disabled suffering from physical and mental challenges. Tell them it's cheaper to house and heal than it is to harass and incarcerate. Our sisters and brothers need our help, and helping others is the American way!

Imagine the difference we will make when every single one of us takes action with love and kindness.

As part of my personal continuing action, I commit to donating 90% of my earnings from any sales of this book to positive, loving solutions for our brothers and sisters who need our help. Together we are a mighty force of love.

Find a way to help in your neighborhood.

Or if you'd rather help Safe Ground, here are some options:

- Snapdragonhealingcenter.com – healing PTSD, bipolar disorder, depression, grief, through art.
- Safegroundsac.org – the original nonprofit born of the Safe Ground movement.
- Firststepcommunities.org – bridge out of homelessness, tiny homes and counseling.

~

We can do this together, with love and understanding. Zero veterans homeless and zero mentally ill homeless! United we stand.

Made in the USA
Las Vegas, NV
15 August 2021